WITHDRAWN

SOCIOECONOMIC METHODS IN
EDUCATIONAL ANALYSIS

SOCIOECONOMIC METHODS IN EDUCATIONAL ANALYSIS

WILLIAM H. WEBER, III

TEACHERS COLLEGE PRESS
TEACHERS COLLEGE, COLUMBIA UNIVERSITY
NEW YORK AND LONDON

LC
65
W42

Copyright © 1975 by Teachers College, Columbia University

Library of Congress Catalog Card Number: 74-28195

Library of Congress Cataloging in Publication Data:

Weber, William H 1933-
  Socioeconomic methods in educational analysis.

  Includes bibliographical references.
  1. Education—Economic aspects. 2. Socialization.
3. System analysis. I. Title.
LC65.W42   301.5'6   74-28195

Manufactured in the United States of America

For my parents

FOREWORD

The twentieth century has witnessed notable development of the several social sciences to their present highly technical and differentiated levels. Anthropology, economics, political science, social psychology, sociology —all have generated their characteristic ways of asking questions, of collecting and ordering data, and of drawing inferences. Above all, each discipline has developed its specialized terminology, as an essential tool for reporting systematic inquiry.

Whatever extension of analytic power this specialization of the social science disciplines may have brought, it has necessarily created one most undesirable side effect: the raising of barriers to communication among practitioners of different disciplines. Truth about social phenomena is sought within the confines of a single discipline; only too often, the contributions of other social sciences are either unknown, or ignored.

The study of education has not escaped this movement toward specialized analysis. What economists have been saying about rates of return to investment in schooling; what anthropologists have done in analyzing the culture of public schools; what sociologists have found out about the linkages among children's educational aspirations, expectations, and attainment; and what political scientists have discovered about the role of schooling in legitimizing and fortifying the governments of newly independent states—all these and other results of scholarly inquiry are commonly couched in the specialized languages of the several social sciences.

Dr. Weber's book shows how some of the basic analytic tools developed by economists can be employed to model a wide variety of educational phenomena. The author demonstrates, I think successfully, that many sociological, anthropological, political, and pedagogical insights concerning the operation of educational systems and institutions can be usefully expressed in the language of dynamically interacting forces. Such systems of forces shift and change through time, sometimes slowly, sometimes rapidly. At times, the movement seems to be toward an equilibrium position (stability); at others, the trend appears to be disequilibrating (destabilizing). Analysis of such situations plays a central role in modern economics, which tries to provide answers to such questions as: Will a given change in a particular variable (say, taxation, employment, incomes, or savings) be stabilizing or destabilizing? What are the conditions under which a given change in a variable will provoke stabilizing or destabilizing reactions in the economic system?

Cognate questions have occurred much less frequently in educational analysis, partly because the problems connected with modeling interactions among educational phenomena seemed so daunting. In this book Dr. Weber shows us that there are ways to overcome the difficulties and that, indeed, students beginning their studies of educational phenomena can be brought to conceptualize the operation of educational systems and institutions in a way that is not only useful in its own right, but has the added merit of making possible a greater degree of communication among the social science disciplines.

Any author who is prepared to reach from Plato's *Republic* to Peter Blau's *Exchange and Power in Social Life,* going by way of Daniel Lerner's *The Passing of Traditional Society* and Jencks' and Riesman's *The Academic Revolution* is clearly not lacking in courage. Dr. Weber is to be congratulated, I feel, for attempting what so many advocate and so few do: move out from the security of one's "home" discipline to range widely beyond its familiar confines. Dr. Weber has done this not only with courage, but with a sure touch and with excellent results. This book will surely be of first importance to all those who wish to improve their powers of conceptualizing system-type interactions among education-related phenomena.

Harold J. Noah

Teachers College, Columbia University
January 1975

INTRODUCTION

ELEMENTS OF SOCIAL SCIENTIFIC METHOD

On a preliminary basis, we may hold that each social science is characterized by a particular method or set of methods of analysis. We associate the comparative method with political science, an association that extends at least as far back as Aristotle's *Politics*. Sociology is set apart by its dependence on social structural analysis and such derivative constructs as functional analysis and the Mertonian thrust through role and status set analysis. Social psychology, although it takes much from sociology, is set apart by its experimental orientation, an infusion from the field's deep roots in experimental psychology. Finally, there is economics, a discipline peculiarly characterized by its method of structuring models of social interdependence and causality through the use of geometric and mathematical representations of series of interconnected functional relationships.

Although there is nothing inherent in any discipline's principal method (or methods) of analysis that limits the use of this methodology to the particular subject matter of interest to the practitioners of a particular discipline, it is, nonetheless, a fact of social scientific life that economists by and large limit their methodological tool kit to those methods commonly employed by other economists, which are not the methods commonly employed by sociologists, political scientists, or social psychologists.

The method of a particular discipline and the concepts and constructs derived through a consistent application of that method structure the existential reality of the practitioners of a discipline, determining what is of interest, structuring the logic of analysis, and limiting the kind and range of questions legitimately posed.

The disciplinary division of labor that has developed in the social sciences (as well as in the physical sciences) appears to be highly efficient. This disciplinary division of labor has resulted in many problem areas' being cast out of bounds by all disciplines because these problem areas fall into boundary areas between the established disciplines and require the fusion of two or more disciplinary methods for their analysis. Education is one such area; international relations is another. The former requires the fusion of methods drawn from economics, sociology, and social psychology, whereas the latter requires both economic and sociological methods and little of the comparative method we are here associating with traditional political science.

The purpose of this book is to explore the possibilities for educational analysis of a fusion of methods drawn from economics, sociology, and social psychology, the resulting synthesis to be called *socioeconomic* analysis. Another purpose, and one equally important, is to teach this method. In the final analysis, the value of any method of inquiry must rest on its productivity. Thus, a third purpose is to demonstrate the productivity of this method through examples of its application. Needless to say, in a book of this length, none of our goals will be fully achieved.

Years as a student and as a teacher of economics indicate that the only way of effectively learning and teaching method is, first, to observe numerous applications of the method and, second, to attempt work in which the method is given a demanding test. Extended discussions of method have never in my experience been very productive among those for whom method is a means and not an end. So it is that the plan of this work is to display the socioeconomic method at work in widely varying educational problem contexts, running the range from an analysis of classroom interaction to the role of higher education in the complex process of societal change.

Education offers a particularly fruitful research area. The problems offered by the institutions and systems of formal education in all societies are both important and difficult. Further, experience indicates that most of the problems encountered in educational contexts are, without difficulty, to be seen in other contexts as well. Placing this thought the other way around, most organizational research, small group research, research on total institutions, etc., has results that suggest educational applications.

THE PLAN OF THE BOOK

Part One: Macrosocietal Considerations

Part One begins with a detailed consideration of the role of education in a society that never existed, *The Republic* of Plato's design. In treating *The Republic*, we demonstrate how socioeconomic analysis may be used to reformulate an existing piece of social analysis and, in reformulating that work, to discover aspects latent in the writer's analysis.

Following *The Republic*, there is an examination of the role assigned to education by Daniel Lerner in *The Passing of Traditional Society*. In the case of Lerner, the focus is not so much on reformulation as it is on technique in model construction using the socioeconomic method. For both Plato and Lerner, the application of the method results in the development of a new perspective and in a greatly compressed representation of selected aspects of the authors' analyses.

The macrosocietal section of the book concludes with the construction of a model that attempts to capture selected aspects of the complex relationships between change in modern societies and the curriculum in institutions of higher education.

Part Two: Microsocietal Considerations

Part Two contains two models, one dealing with the curricular implications at all levels of formal education of changes in conditions of supply and demand for teachers, and one detailing some of the dynamics of change in higher education in the United States during the 1960's.

Part Three: Organization Theoretic Considerations

Organization Development (OD) is an applied aspect of the discipline of social psychology and is of growing importance in that field. Part Three opens with a model designed to detail selected aspects of the social dynamics within a school. The model is normative in that it posits a desirable state for an educational institution and a means for achieving that state. Part Three closes with a detailed analysis of teacher-student interaction in a classroom within the context of a course, that is, within the context of a series of meetings between a teacher and a group of students. The model of teacher-student interaction differs from all previous models in this book in that explicitly economic constructs are extensively used in its development.

SOME CONCLUDING NOTES

Readership

Given the method and plan of this book, readers of this Introduction may be somewhat uncertain about the audience to whom this book is addressed. Readers with an interest in (and some upper-level preparation in) sociology, social psychology, or economics should find this work of particular interest. Hopefully, the book will serve to recruit young social scientists to the task of educational analysis, an area of research that has too long suffered from a lack of individual social scientific research initiatives.

The Way of the Work

Having been deeply socialized into the discipline of economics, it has taken a number of years for this writer to dissociate the method of economics from the subject matter of economics, and yet more years to accumulate a sufficient knowledge of sociology and social psychology to reach a point where movement between these fields has about it *some* feeling of comfort.

A great debt is owed those individuals mentioned in the Acknowledgments, but a quite unique debt is owed to the many students who have demonstrated their ability to creatively apply the approach developed here, many of whom were relatively or totally ignorant of both parent disciplines, economics and sociology.

ACKNOWLEDGMENTS

When a social investigator addresses the subject of method, he is ever conscious of his indebtedness to those who have communicated a store of established and, in some cases, not so established method to him, out of which he has developed his own set of ordering constructs, and for which set of ordering constructs he alone is to be held accountable.

For their personal efforts to communicate scholarship, discipline, and method, I am in great debt to Eirik G. Furubotn, Harold J. Noah, Peter M. Blau, Robert K. Merton, James M. Buchanan, and Gordon Tullock. Others who have spoken to me strongly but mainly, or exclusively, through their writings are Karl Polanyi, Talcott Parsons, Amitai Etzioni, and Karl R. Popper.

Drawing together several disciplines takes an extended period of study. For the unusual quality and degree of her support in this enterprise, I owe more than I can express to my wife, Gail. And for their unquestioning moral and financial support through the years of study, I am most happy to single out my parents.

I think it safe to say that writing on method is the least safe of all academic undertakings, and the next would have to be publishing such writings. For their support, in these financially difficult times, of books dealing with subjects of some considerable controversy, I must acknowledge Teachers College Press. And finally, for her careful editing and advice, I acknowledge the valuable help of my editor, Janet M. Simons. Appreciation is also due Agnes Scott College for the assistance provided by a faculty research grant.

CONTENTS

Foreword by *Harold J. Noah*   v

Introduction   vii

Acknowledgments   xi

Part One
MACROSOCIETAL CONSIDERATIONS

Chapter I
The Role of Education in Plato's *Republic*   3

Chapter II
Technological Change, Social Change, and the Higher Education Curriculum   18

Chapter III
Literacy in a Model of Low-Level Equilibrium   32

Part Two
MICROSOCIETAL CONSIDERATIONS

Chapter IV
A Socioeconomic Model of the Determinants of
the Conceptual Level of the Curriculum   45

Chapter V
Functional Prerequisites in an Equilibrium Model
of the United States System of Higher Education   54

Part Three
ORGANIZATION THEORETIC CONSIDERATIONS

Chapter VI
A Model of Organizational Development
Applied to a School   81

Chapter VII
A Socioeconomic Model of Classroom Communication   94

Postscript   117

Index of Names   121

Index of Subjects   123

Part One
MACROSOCIETAL CONSIDERATIONS

Chapter I

THE ROLE OF EDUCATION IN PLATO'S REPUBLIC

In this chapter, we will analyze the function of the educational system Plato built into his *Republic*, within his assumptions about the nature of social relationships; demonstrate the usefulness of socioeconomic model-building techniques in the analysis of the internal logic of models constructed utilizing the classical literary approach; and introduce the reader to the socioeconomic method.

First, it might be well to point out why *The Republic* is considered a model in the literary tradition. An analysis is a model if it is a succinct statement of theory, that is, a logically coherent system of causal relationships. Our examination of Plato's work will demonstrate the way in which it conforms to the "succinct statement" criterion.[1]

---

[1] Joseph A. Schumpeter was of two minds concerning the analytical nature of *The Republic*. At one point in his *History of Economic Analysis* (New York: Oxford University Press, 1954), he says, "The picture he painted of the Perfect State in his Politeia [*The Republic*] is no more analysis than a painter's rendering of a Venus is scientific anatomy." He goes on to note, however, that Plato's "idea of the Perfect State is cor-

The type of model Plato constructed is a stabilized stationary state system, and, in addition, it is a normative model because the analysis is clearly directed by a desire to mirror the form-of-state Plato thought ought to be approximated by actual states. Through *The Republic*, Plato attempts to demonstrate that his beliefs concerning values are really knowledge; that is, that the values he holds can be shown to be in the best interest of the individual, which, as he reasons, also represents the best interest of the State.

In this socioeconomic reformulation of Plato's model, the philosophical issues he raises will not be our concern. Our attention will be directed toward the issue of the role played by education in achieving a stabilized stationary condition for his Perfect State; for if *The Republic* is the platonic form of the state, then it must be at once both perfect and changeless.

Plato makes three points at the outset of his analysis: (1) A condition of Justice is the goal of the State. Ranked with, but also part of, Justice are the goals of Wisdom, Courage, and Temperance. (2) Nature drives men together, and in the course of events it is discovered that specialization within a social function or occupation yields an increase in social and material benefits. The welfare of the individual and of the group is maximized when each individual does that sub-task within one of the social tasks for which Nature has suited him. (3) As long as the state is small and isolated, specialization will not be very great, and, therefore, the economic, political, and military organization of the state will be quite simple. Such states are inherently unstable, and will either die out or become more complex.

According to Plato's analysis, the drive to increased complexity is a result of the efforts of those in the group with a taste for luxury to increase their level of material comfort. The desire for luxury cannot be satisfied without a substantial increase in the economic base. This increase requires the division of labor (occupational specialization), the accumulation of capital (producers' goods), and an expansion of the market through foreign trade.

With increased economic complexity comes a need for the most elemental kinds of social capital (public goods) such as streets and roads, a water system, defense, control of minting (a monetary system must replace the barter system if occupational specialization is to develop), and the setting of standards of weights and measures. The collection of taxes to pay for these public goods calls forth a demand for a

---

related with the material furnished by the observation of actual states. And there is no reason whatever to deny the analytic or scientific character . . . of such observations . . ." (p. 55).

more formal system of government. Knowing that these things must come to be, Plato set about designing the Perfect Complex State, *The Republic*.

Into his Perfect State, Plato has built what he considers the necessary and sufficient conditions for the attainment of Justice. Based on certain assumptions concerning the distribution of abilities within a given population (which, in turn, are based upon certain genetic assumptions), he concluded that a small percentage of the population will be capable of producing wisdom and that such individuals will, by and large, have children who also will have this capacity. Plato thought that a slightly larger percentage of the people would be capable of producing acts of Courage or Spirit, and that such people would bear spirited children. Finally, Plato believed that the majority of the citizens would be Appetitive, driven by material gain, and would have offspring who also responded to the lure of material gain.

Plato thought that the Perfect State would need to have three basic functions performed: Government, Defense, and Economy. To each of the basic social functions he assigned one of his "character types": to the governing function he assigned those capable of Wisdom, to the defense function he assigned the Spirited, and to the economic function he assigned the Appetitive. Few are needed in the governing function, say 5%, a larger percentage are needed for defense, say 20%, and most are needed for the economy, say 75%. Inasmuch as the number of people required for each of the three functions naturally occurs in the population, there is a balance between the needs of the state and what Nature provides.

As has been mentioned, Justice is the goal of the State. This goal is achieved when the rulers (the Guardians) have Wisdom; when the defenders of the State (the Auxiliaries) exhibit Courage; and when the economic class (the Tradesmen), the rulers, and the defenders all exhibit Temperance. Temperance is agreement by all that reason must rule, that the class system reflects reason, and that each individual is placed in that class intended for him by Nature (or, as Plato would have all but the Guardians believe, by the gods).

Education is the means by which each citizen in each class is socialized into and prepared for his class function. The system of Education must be so effective that no citizen can even conceive of his performing the duties of one in another class. Thus did Plato expect to eliminate class conflict in the Perfect State. Because Plato had observed the instability that class conflict produced in actual states, he was most concerned with its total control, and it is for this reason that such a large proportion of *The Republic* is devoted to a detailed discussion of the particulars of his curriculum.

6 SOCIOECONOMIC METHODS

A SOCIOECONOMIC MODEL OF *THE REPUBLIC*

The Nature of Models in the Social Sciences

Before introducing the model, we will undertake a short discussion of the term *model*. Following are four definitions of the term, moving from the most general to the most specific:

1. A model is a succinct statement of theory.[2]
2. A model is a logically coherent system of causal relationships.
3. A model is a group or set of social relationships, each one of which involves at least one variable that also appears in at least one other relationship, such that in one relationship the variable is independent and in the other it is dependent.[3] For example, "Education" may appear as a variable, the level of which is determined by the interaction of several variables considered to be independent variables in relation to "Education." "Education" must also be a causal or independent variable somewhere else in the system of causal relationships, however. In this way, "Education" becomes a link in a complex set of interdependencies.
4. A model is (a) a list of variables and (b) a list of relationships or equations specifying the links of any type that are hypothesized to exist between the variables. The list of relationships is usually divided into (i) definitional identities; (ii) balance equations, or statements of central tendencies within the system, such as quantity supplied tends to equal quantity demanded ($S=D$); (iii) technological or institutional equations, an example being an equation stating that the level of government spending is a function of the level of unemployment, a policy relationship established as a result of the Full Employment Act of 1946; and (iv) behavioral equations, such as quantity demanded of X falls as a function of, as a result of, increases in the price of X.[4]

The List of Variables

Following the procedure outlined in the Tinbergen-Bos definition (the fourth definition above), we present a list of the variables and their definitions for the Plato model:

1. $E =$ Education. Education refers to the formal process through

---

[2] Adapted from Gardner Ackley, *Macroeconomic Theory* (New York: Macmillan, 1961), pp. 12-14.
[3] *Ibid*.
[4] Adapted from Jan Tinbergen and Hendricks C. Bos, *Mathematical Models of Economic Growth* (New York: McGraw-Hill, 1962), p. 6.

which knowledge and beliefs are communicated. The type, content, and method of education used in *The Republic* are determined by Plato's ruling class. The amount of community resources directed to education is determined by the model; that is, it is an endogenously determined variable.
2. $P=$ The Population of the State.
3. $U=$ Urbanization. Urbanization refers "to that cumulative accentuation of the characteristics distinctive of the mode of life which is associated with the growth of cities . . . ."[5]
4. $O_s=$ Occupational Specialization. Occupational Specialization is the division of labor in the performance of the economic tasks of the State.
5. $RFS=$ Required Functional Specialization. *RFS* refers to the development of well-defined classes that specialize in carrying out the various needs of the State. Plato saw these functional needs as government, military, and economy.[6]
6. $AFS=$ Actual Functional Specialization. *AFS* refers to the achieved degree of functional separation of prerequisite tasks.
7. $Y=$ The total Value of Goods and Services Produced by the Community in One Year and Available for Investment or Consumption.
8. $AP=$ Average Product. *AP* is defined as Y/P.
9. $PG=$ Public Goods. Public Goods are services and facilities that when produced and/or made available tend to benefit broad segments of the population of the State. Because of the broad-based benefits attaching to the provision of Public Goods and the difficulty or impossibility of excluding citizens from the benefits produced, these goods and services are financed through taxes rather than through sale in markets.

Section One of the Model

THE FUNCTIONAL RELATIONSHIPS

We will first discuss the functional relationships linking variables 2, 3, 4, 7, and 8. In the statement of any functional, or causal, relationship

---

[5] Louis Wirth, "Urbanism as a Way of Life," in Albert J. Reiss, Jr., ed., *Lewis Wirth on Cities and Social Life* (Chicago: University of Chicago Press, 1964), p. 64.
[6] The notion of Required Functional Specialization is clear in *The Republic*, but it is also a critically important part of modern sociology as it appears in the form of structural-functional analysis developed by Talcott Parsons. The approach to societal analysis through structural-functional analysis holds that any human society has functional prerequisites or jobs that, if not done (or performed), will result in the dissolution of the social system. The functions Plato saw as necessary to the stability of the State, or prerequisite to its stability, were Government based on Rationality and Wisdom, Defense based on the virtue of Courage, and Economy motivated by Private Interest. The structure charged with the performance of these functions was a Class System.

8   SOCIOECONOMIC METHODS

hypothesized to exist between variables, there is an assumption that the exact nature of the relationship depends upon the value of certain variables that, for purposes of the analysis, are assumed to be constant in value. Such conditioning and constant valued variables are known as parameters. Because Plato did not indicate the parametric conditions associated with his hypothesized functional relationships, with two critical exceptions, we cannot add them. (In the models that follow this chapter, the parametric conditions will be discussed.) Quotations from the Jowett translation of *The Republic* will be used to illustrate the way in which Plato's observations have been embodied in each of the following functional relationships:

1. $O_s = f(U)$. Occupational Specialization is a function of, is systematically related to and caused by, the level of Urbanization. "And will you have a work better done when the workman has many occupations, or when he has only one? When he has only one. . . . Then more than four citizens will be required; for the husbandman will not make his own plough or mattock, or other implements of agriculture, if they are to be good for anything." [Bk. II, 370]
2. $AP = f(O_s)$. Average Product is a function of the degree of Occupational Specialization. ". . . we must infer that all things are produced more plentifully and easily and of better quality when one man does one thing which is natural to him and does it at the right time, and leaves other things." [Bk. II, 370]
3. $P = f(AF)$. Population is a function of Average Product, *ceteris paribus*.[7] "Now will the city have to fill and swell with a multitude of callings which are not required by any natural want. . . ." [Bk. II, 373]
4. $U = f(P)$. Urbanization is a function of Population. "For I suspect that many will not be satisfied with the simpler way of life. They will be for adding sofas, and tables, and other furniture; also dainties, and perfumes, and incense, and courtesans, and cakes, all these not of one sort only, but in every variety. . . ." [Bk. II, 373]

THE MODEL

These four functional relationships are illustrated in graphic form in Figure 1. The figure attempts to show how the four relationships are linked in a causal sequence. In Part A of Figure 1, the level of Urbanization that will result from any given level of Population is specified by

---

[7] The term *ceteris paribus* means "other things being equal"; it indicates that there are important parametric conditions that need to be discussed.

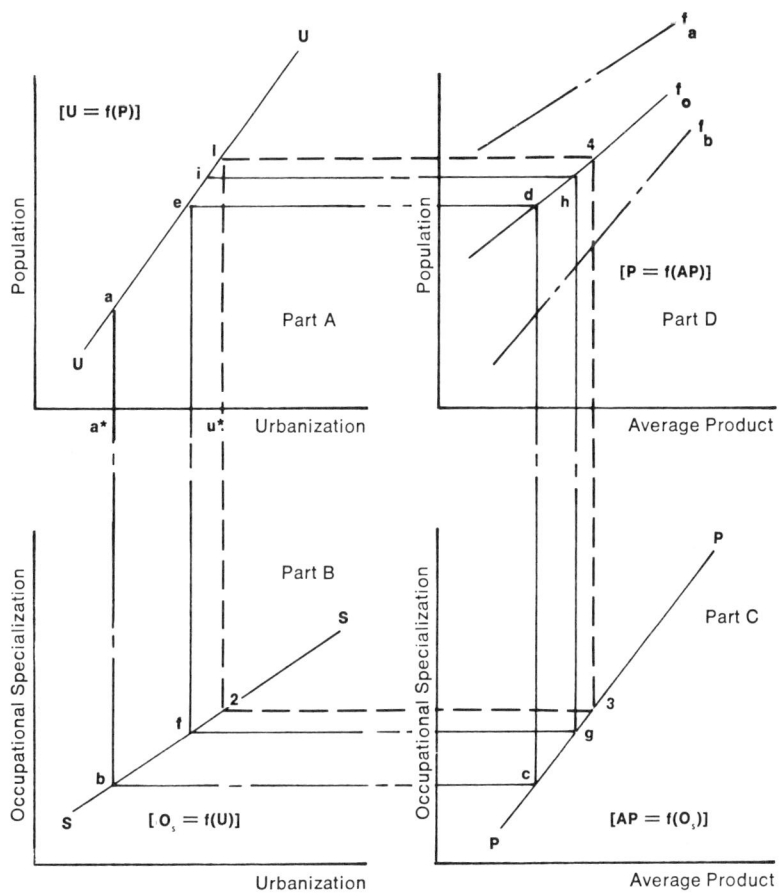

FIGURE 1. Model of *The Republic*: Section One

Curve UU, the Urbanization Function. The curve, or function, is the locus of coordinates that satisfy the equation $U=f(P)$, when the equation is stated in a mathematically specific manner rather than in the general form used here. Because Plato gives no indication as to how the slope of the curve might change over the range of the variables, but only indicates the direction (positive or negative association between increases in the causal and induced changes in the caused, or dependent, variable), the functions of this model are shown by curves of constant slope.

The system illustrated by Figure 1 is a type of dynamic model in which the broken lines indicate the path generated over time by the interaction of the functional relationships. In Part A, the a level of Population will eventually cause the level of Urbanization to rise to (or fall to, depending upon the direction of population change) the a^* level, as indicated on the horizontal axis of Part A. The a^* level of Urbanization requires that Occupational Specialization rise (or fall, as the case may be) to the b level, as indicated in Part B, where the Specialization Function specifies the level of O_s that will come to be associated with any given level of Urbanization. As Plato indicates, Urbanization is a process attended by a rise in the level of wants that go beyond those he considers natural. As this level of wants increases, it becomes possible for men to specialize, not only because more things and a greater variety of things are wanted, but also because the larger market for things permits an individual to live by producing only one thing or part of a thing. As Adam Smith was to note some centuries later, specialization is limited by the extent of the market.

In Part C we see that the b level of O_s will eventually cause the level of Average Product to settle (up or down) to the c level of AP. The relationship between Occupational Specialization and Average Product is, in Tinbergen and Bos' terms, a technological one; thus, the PP Curve, the Productivity Function, is not a behavioral function, is not determined by the operation of spontaneous societal forces reflecting the culture of the people (as is the case with the functions shown in Parts A and B). Rather, it is technological, reflecting the fact that O_s will always be accompanied by the development of refined methods of production leading to an increase in physical productivity.

So far as Plato was concerned, or so far as can be discovered from reading *The Republic*, the functional relationships shown in Parts A, B, and C were beyond the control of the rulers. The function subject to policy variation by the Guardians (and therefore could be used by them to control the dynamic process) is the one that relates the level of Population to the level of Average Product. It is for this reason that the statement of the functional relationship $P=f(AP)$ ended with the expression *ceteris paribus*. To indicate that the f Function, relating P to AP, can be shifted to any position desired by the Guardians, Part D shows not one curve but three.

It is very clear that Plato was quite concerned about the size of the population of his State:

> And what, I said, will be the best limit for our rulers to fix when they are considering the size of the State and the amount of territory which they are to include, and beyond which they will not go? What limit would you propose?

EDUCATION IN PLATO'S *REPUBLIC* 11

I would allow the State to increase so far as is consistent with unity; that, I think, is the proper limit.

Very good, he said.

Here then, I said, is another order which will have to be conveyed to our Guardians: Let our city be accounted neither large nor small, but one and self-sufficing. [Bk. IV, 423]

To control population growth, Plato developed an elaborate set of myths. In operation, these myths, as used by the Guardians and taught by the educational system, would not only control the birth rate but also result in breeding by scientific selection:

I mean, I replied, that our rulers will find a considerable dose of falsehood and deceit necessary for the good of their subjects. . . . [Bk. V, 459]

Had we not better appoint certain festivals at which we will bring together the brides and the bridegrooms . . . the number of weddings is a matter which must be left to the discretion of the rulers, whose aim will be to preserve the average of the population? There are other things which they will have to consider, such as the effects of wars and diseases and any similar agencies, in order as far as this is possible to prevent the State from becoming either too large or too small.

Certainly, he replied.

We shall have to invent some ingenious kind of lots which the less worthy may draw on each occasion of our bringing them together, and then they will accuse their own ill-luck and not the rulers. [Bk. V, 460]

Thus, through myths taught in school and State-managed religious festivals, Plato sought to give the Guardians control over the natural relationship between a rising per capita income and a growth in population. By shifting the f Function, it is also possible to control the level of Occupational Specialization and the level of Urbanization, as will become clear as the model is further developed.

In Part C, the c level of Average Product will, with the passage of time, cause the level of Population to rise to the d level, on the assumption that it is the f_o Function that is effective and not either the f_a or the f_b Function.

By following this path through several more iterations, the process whereby the State grows can be illustrated. A careful inspection of the size of the increases in the variables as the expansion continues indicates that the process slows over time until the value of each variable is such that no further expansion is possible. The coordinates numbered 1, 2, 3, and 4 indicate the stable set of values of the variables; u^*, indicated on the horizontal axis of Part A, is the desired situation, a State neither too small nor too large, one self-sustaining at a satisfactory level of luxury.

Section Two of the Model

THE FUNCTIONAL RELATIONSHIPS

The functional relationships of Section Two deal with the social structural aspects of the State. The variables employed in these relationships are, with one exception, those not employed in the development of Section One. The exception is Urbanization, for it is the level of Urbanization that dictates the configuration of the social structure:

1. $RFS = f(U)$. Required Functional Specialization is a function of the level of Urbanization. One example of this relationship is given by Plato in his discussion of the need for a class of citizens devoted entirely to the defense needs of the State. The State requires additional farm land to support a growing population; thus the army is not only for defense, but is also needed for territorial expansion: "The territory of our State must be enlarged; and hence will arise war between us and our neighbors" [Bk. II, 373]. "War is an art, and as no art can be pursued with success unless a man's whole attention is devoted to it, a soldier cannot be allowed to exercise any calling but his own" [Bk. II, 374]. The optimal degree of Urbanization (Point u^* on the horizontal axis of Part A in Figure 1) is determined by Plato to be that level of Urbanization requiring exactly three classes for the creation of a condition of Unity within the State. This is so because Nature has structured mankind to provide the conditions essential to Justice under a three-class system.
2. $PG = f(U)$. Public Goods and Services provided by the Rulers are determined in kind and amount by the level of Urbanization. "[A means whereby the goods and services produced by those who are occupationally specialized can be exchanged is essential to the process of occupational specialization itself, and to] . . . secure such an exchange was, as you will remember, one of the principal objects when we formed them into a society and constituted a State. Clearly they will buy and sell. Then they will need a market-place, and a money-token for purposes of exchange" [Bk. II, 371].

3. $E=f(PG)$. Education, or the resources of the State devoted to education, is a function of the overall level of Public Goods provision. Education is a Public Good of extreme importance in Plato's State. Plato discusses "The Education of Heroes," the "Training for Warrior Athletes," "The True Aim of Music and Gymnastic," the "Selection and Education of Soldiers," the "Education for Women," "The Training of the Rulers," and "The Mental Training Given by Arithmetic." In addition, there are many paragraphs devoted to the philosophy of education. The large investment in educational facilities and the large current costs of operating these facilities are left implicit; from what we are told, however, it would seem that these facilities must be hidden from adult view: "They are to be told that their youth was a dream, and the education and training which they received from us [from the rulers], an appearance only; in reality during all that time they were being formed and fed in the womb of the earth, where they themselves and their arms and appurtenances were manufactured . . ." [Bk. III, 414]. The extraordinary myth concerning the reality of the citizens' educational experience is all part of Plato's scheme to avoid class conflict, to achieve the virtue of Temperance within each class.
4. $AFS=f(E)$. Actual Functional Specialization is a function of Education, *ceteris paribus*. This relationship is true by design; that is, it is the purpose of Education to bring the Required degree of Functional Specialization into being. If the educational system is not operating correctly, however, the AFS may differ from the RFS.
5. $AFS=RFS$. Actual Functional Specialization tends to equal the Required Functional Specialization.

If our model were what in economics is known as a stable equilibrium system, Equation 5 would be termed the balance equation; it would specify the basic tendency of the spontaneous operation of the system. In the case of Plato's model, which is a stabilized stationary state system, Equation 5 is an institutional equation, giving the goal toward which the Ruling Class, the Institution, is constantly moving. If we apply the Tinbergen-Bos classification of types of functional relationships to Equations 1 through 5, we note that Equation 1 is, as Plato sees it, a behavioral equation; it represents a relationship that is determined out of the spontaneous operation of a society within a particular cultural context. Equation 2, which may be thought of as a statement of the determinants of the demand for Public Goods, is also a behavioral equation, as is Equation 3, Education as a type of Public Good. Equation 4

14 SOCIOECONOMIC METHODS

is a technological-institutional equation, and the Rulers, through their control over Education, can adjust this functional relationship to achieve their goal, which is to create a Just State by bringing about Equation 5. $RFS = AFS$.

THE MODEL

Equations 1 through 4 are graphically specified in Parts E through H of Figure 2. The optimal level of Urbanization, u^*, is indirectly determined by the RR Function of Part E; that is, the 5 level of RFS is that level at

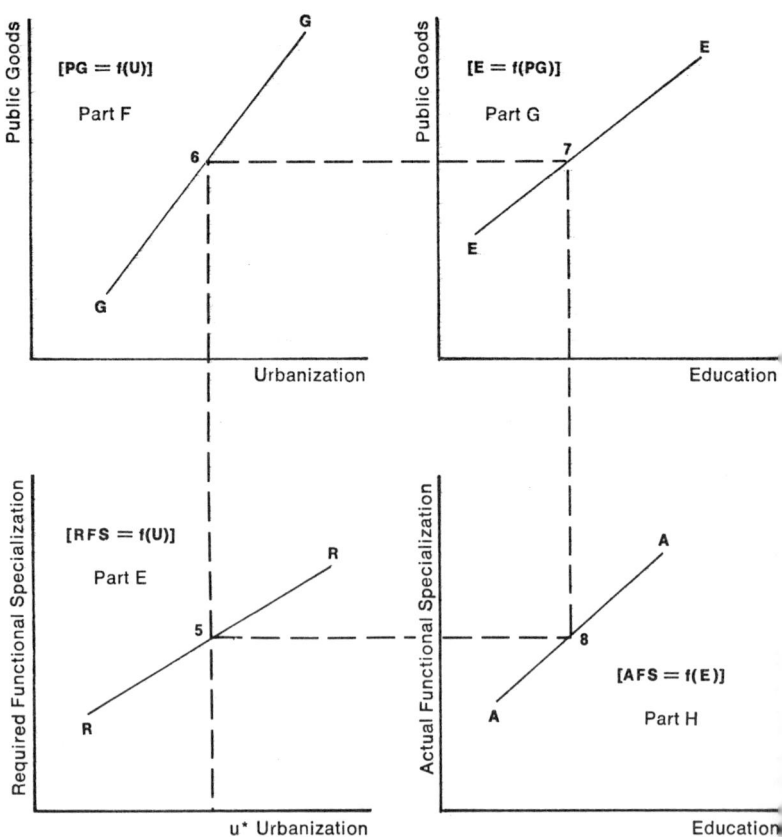

FIGURE 2. Model of *The Republic:* Section Two

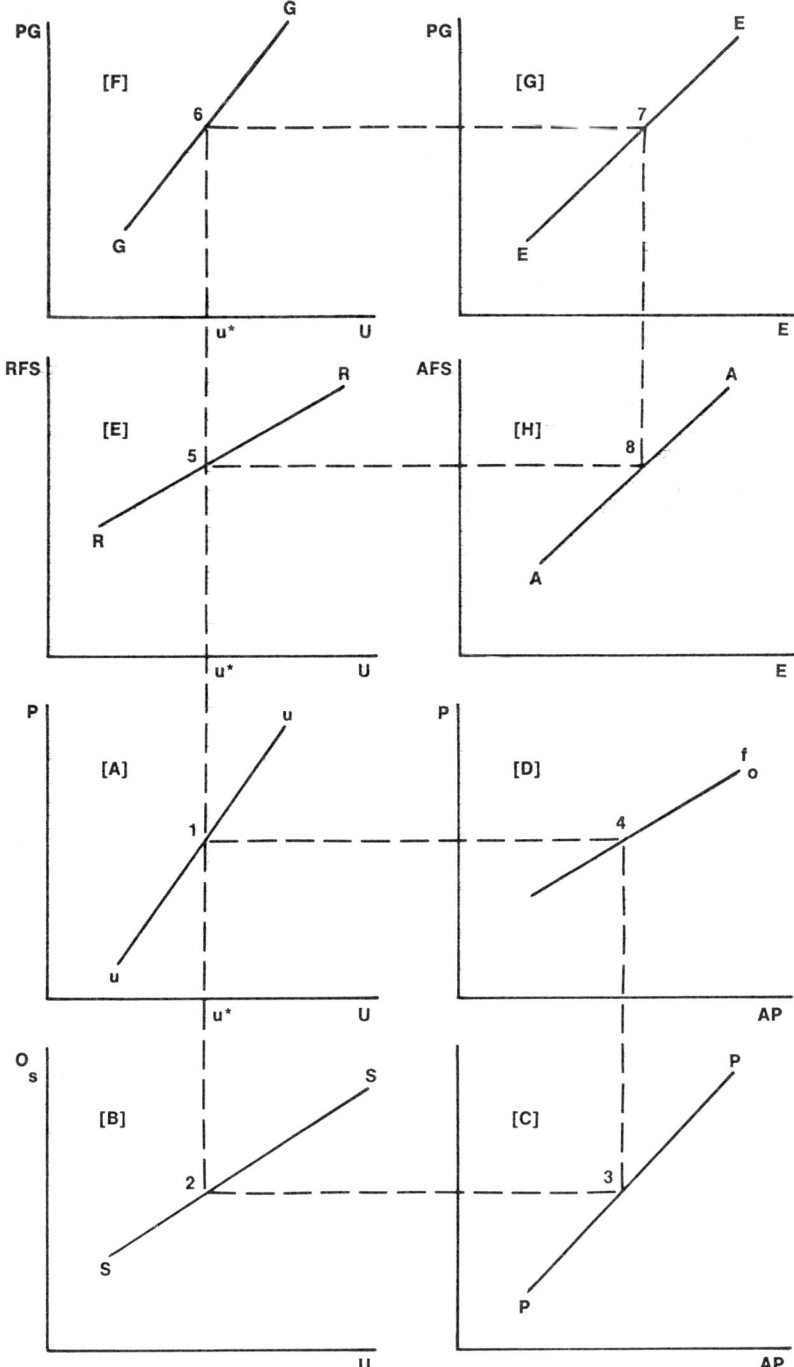

FIGURE 3. Model of *The Republic*

which the three-class system is required, and although it is Urbanization that determines *RFS*, it is Plato's understanding of the structural requirements for Justice that determines the desired level of *RFS*. Given that level of *RFS*, we can then determine the level of Urbanization consistent with the desired *RFS*. The optimal level of Urbanization is then made an input into Section One, indicating to the Rulers where the f Function of Part D must be positioned to achieve a stabilized state at the u^* level of Urbanization.

The u^* level of Urbanization will generate a demand for Public Goods of Level 6, shown on the *GG* Function of Part F in Figure 2. The 6 level of *PG* Demand has, as a part of that demand, the 7 level of Education, as shown on the *EE* Function of Part G. In Part H, the 7 level of Education requires positioning the *AA* Function in such a way that the 7 level of Education causes *AFS* to achieve Level 8, shown on the *AA* Function. As the second section of the model indicates, achieving the 8 level of *AFS* meets the goal set for the Guardians by Plato of bringing *RFS* into equality with *AFS*; the 8 level of *AFS* is equal to the 5 level of *RFS*.

Both sections of the Socioeconomic Model of *The Republic* have now been completed. The two sections are shown together in Figure 3. As must be clear, it is the method and content of the education given to the citizens of the State that permit the Rulers to shift the *AA* Function of Part H and the f Function of Part D so that the stationary state system is stabilized, thereby bringing about the conditions necessary to the creation of Justice. Is it any wonder then that so much of Plato's thought was directed to the educational system of his Perfect State!

In *The Republic,* Plato discusses some of the forms of government he has observed in actual states, including democracy, oligarchy, and tyranny. Viewed from the position of our model, Plato's criticism of these forms of government reduces to the simple conclusion that these real world forms are unstable because in each the Required level of Functional Specialization exceeds the Actual level of Functional Specialization.

SOME CONCLUDING COMMENTS

Readers unfamiliar with the model-building techniques of economics will, doubtless, have found the analysis presented in this chapter somewhat difficult to follow. Experience indicates that this is to be expected, and experience also indicates that, although subsequent models are more complex than this one, the reader will find them progressively easier to understand.

The socioeconomic method of model construction has imposed upon Plato's work a degree of exactness he could scarcely have intended. If the model has been constructed with care, however, the essential logic of the literary model has been retained and, in addition, much that was implicit in the literary model has been made explicit. In the case of *The Republic*, it has been made manifest through the socioeconomic method that, when taken together, Plato's observations concerning behavioral relationships and his assumptions concerning the nature of man do indeed compose a logically coherent system. One need not agree with Plato's assumptions about the nature of man, or believe his behavioral observations to be accurate, to appreciate the fact that in *The Republic* we have an example of modern model building of a very high order, a fact that has not heretofore been recognized.[8] This fact is demonstrated by our ability to construct, in geometric form, utilizing the socioeconomic method, a model consisting of a logically coherent system of causal relationships based on the verbal form given these relationships by Plato in *The Republic*.

[8] Alvin W. Gouldner, *Enter Plato: Classical Greece and the Origins of Social Theory* (New York: Basic Books, 1965), sees Plato as, in part, a model builder, but he does not actually build Plato's model. Concerning Plato's "Model-Guided Strategy of Change," Gouldner says, "the assumption is that every problem has only one best solution, that the planner should aim to determine what it is and strive to attain it, so far as he can" (p. 281). Gouldner goes on to point out some of the problems with the normative approach to social model building.

Chapter II

TECHNOLOGICAL CHANGE, SOCIAL CHANGE, AND THE HIGHER EDUCATION CURRICULUM

Plato's *Republic* was but the first of a continuing series of studies that have investigated the relationship between education and the dynamics of socioeconomic change, development, and stability. There are any number of modern studies that have attempted to establish a relationship between the curricular pattern of a nation and that nation's stage of cultural, social, political, and/or economic development.[1] Many investigators have attempted, through the use of statistical methods, to establish the existence of a relationship between secondary and college enrollment as a percent of age-group and the stage of development of a nation. Statis-

---

[1] In the following chapter, one such study will be subjected to close analysis—Daniel Lerner's *The Passing of Traditional Society* (Glencoe: The Free Press, 1958). Other examples of such studies or collections of such studies to which the reader might refer are Edward E. Denison, *Why Growth Rates Differ* (Washington: The Brookings Institution, 1967); James S. Coleman (ed.), *Education and Political Development* (Princeton: Princeton University Press, 1965); and A. H. Halsey, J. Floud, and C. A. Anderson (eds.), *Education, Economy and Society: A Reader in the Sociology of Education* (New York: The Free Press, 1961). The journal literature in the area is quite vast, with all the social sciences being strongly represented, particularly economics and sociology.

THE HIGHER EDUCATION CURRICULUM 19

tical methods have also been employed to test for an association between stage of development and curricular composition. The technique used is generally cross-sectional statistical analysis, although some studies do employ time-series analysis. Underlying most of the statistical analyses are the following hypotheses: (1) increases in the average level of education, or in basic literacy rates, cause increases in economic productivity; (2) increases in productivity enable and cause increased investment; (3) increased investment leads to the creation of additional jobs requiring higher levels of education; (4) increased demand for educated individuals raises the returns to individual investment in education; (5) increased returns to education cause an increase in the number of people seeking education for themselves and for their children; and (6) the process implied by the first five hypotheses repeats itself again and again, thereby explaining the process of development. Thus, through iterations of this model, a country reaches an advanced stage of development. As the stage of development rises, the educational needs of the country undergo a systematic change, which is reflected in curricular change. There are a number of variations on this model, variations that, for the most part, call for government intervention to ensure the correct supply of educated individuals:

> No country today can rely completely upon market forces to provide the incentives for its people to engage in the kinds of activities most critically needed for development. In some cases, the status and compensation of engineers and scientists are too low. . . . Thus, all countries must take some deliberate measures to influence the allocation of manpower, and these measures may range from outright compulsion to various kinds of financial and nonfinancial inducements.[2]

During the early phases of development, it may be quite appropriate to operate with a model in which none but economic (materialistic) factors are considered, particularly if the model of the society is normative, is a succinct statement of the theory underlying a centrally imposed plan for industrialization. There are, however, many critics who argue that, without regard to the level of development of a society, a model that does not include the operation of non-materialistic factors is one that, if used as the basis for government plans, is bound to produce unexpected and unanticipated results:

---

[2] Frederick Harbison and Charles A. Myers, *Education, Manpower and Economic Growth: Strategies of Human Resource Development* (New York: McGraw-Hill, 1964), p. 175.

There is, perhaps, a general tendency to accord to the schools a "central" position in strategies designed to facilitate economic development. To some extent this reflects an appreciation of the relative lack of alternative institutions that can be utilized, but it stems partially from the notion that schools are particularly manipulable institutions. It is widely believed that schools can readily be modified to meet new economic needs and, more particularly, to accord with the intentions of social and economic planners.[3]

The basic problem with most research and planning efforts intended to bring the education sector into the overall development plan is that the planners begin with a very inadequate model of the causal actualities of the social system (society) they are attempting to influence. Perhaps this is because the planners are more arrested by their visions of how things might be than they are drawn to a careful consideration of the dynamics of the existing system, out of which they must construct the new order:

> The Model-Guided Strategy of Change begins by attempting to clarify what would be ideally desirable rather than first attempting to provide an adaptation to the status quo. It tries to minimize those features of the status quo which are taken as given and to reduce the constraints within which it must plan. Its underlying attitude is, in this respect: why settle for less than the best; why cling to the past. This strategy has a readiness to make a great break with the present and with things as they are; it rejects, at least in the beginning, considerations of "practicality." Since "the way things are" is not felt to be as important as a clarification of the way they should be, it is less disposed to engage in systematic empirical study of existent social arrangements and more inclined toward a primarily intellectual clarification of the projected future rearrangement.[4]

In the area of planned social change, we are very much limited by the existing set of social institutions and by the social mechanisms through which these institutions are connected. It is our position that the relative lack of attention planners pay to the careful analysis of the status quo is accounted for not so much by indifference to and disaffection from the present system as by the absence of a well-developed and widely shared

---

[3] P. J. Foster, "The Vocational School Fallacy in Development Planning," in Mark Blaug (ed.), *Economics of Education 1* (Baltimore: Penguin Books, Inc., 1968), p. 398.
[4] Gouldner, *Enter Plato*, p. 281.

method of socioeconomic analysis. That is, the planners are almost always from the established disciplines—teams of social scientists among whom there is no shared and linking social analytic method.

The model we now develop is designed to illustrate the type of social analysis that should precede any effort to achieve sociopolitically determined goals through centralized planning. The model itself is nonnormative; it attempts to reflect the essential nature of the present system in Western society at the macrosocietal level. Its construction is motivated, however, by a desire to influence the future state of the society through means that call first for an understanding of the critical interrelationships governing the present. In structuring these critical interrelationships, we work from the assumption that a combination of economic and social forces in association with educational institutions, both formal and informal, determines the course along which the society will move.

The reader should recall that one of the primary purposes of this study is to teach the socioeconomic method of social analysis. The method was called into being for the specific purpose of analyzing education and the role of educational systems, both formal and informal, in the dynamics of social change. Thus, it is part of our methodological stance that systems be conceptualized to include the educational sector of the society, which has been systematically excluded from most social science simply because its inclusion tends to require the combined application of methods and constructs drawn from both economics and sociology. The model we develop in this chapter is highly speculative, but it nonetheless serves all our purposes: it illustrates the combined use of methods and constructs from economics and sociology; it details a possible set of interrelationships between higher education and social change at a level of generalization that should interest both historians and policy-oriented social scientists; and it is a logical development of the Plato model, that is, it parallels and extends the techniques introduced in the construction of the Plato model.

Economists are quite familiar with the heuristic usefulness of the assumption that, in any system or subsystem, there is a tendency to equilibrium. This assumption serves the economist in much the same way as the assumption of functional prerequisites serves the sociologist; both are methodological stances or orientations that perform a directing and ordering service, and both figure importantly in this model, just as both were important in the construction of the Plato model.

Although there are many types of equilibrium states recognized by the economist model builder, his first approximations are often organized on the assumption that there exists a systematic set of interrelationships among certain critical variables such that, in the absence of exogenous disturbances (in the absence of parametric change), there is a tendency toward a stationary state within the system, a state in which no further changes occur because of imbalances between the values of the variables. This is illustrated by the stationary or static state in Plato's *Republic,* which required that Actual Functional Specialization be equal to Required Functional Specialization, and by the classic model of supply and demand, in which the quantity demanded tends to equal the quantity supplied, a tendency spontaneously generated by movements in price. In the model developed here it is this assumption, the assumption of equilibrium search by the system, that determined the particular set of functional relationships we hypothesize to connect the higher education curriculum with technological change and social change.

THE ASSUMPTIONS OF THE MODEL

The assumptions of the model shown in Figure 4 are as follows:

1. In advanced Western countries, the composition of the higher education curriculum, defined as the division of offerings between subjects of a highly specialized nature and offerings of a general-integrative nature, is related to the rate of technological and social change.[5]
2. There is a specifiable relationship between the percentage of offerings of a specialized nature and the supportable rate of technological change.[6]
3. Given the determined rate of technological change, there is a rate of specialization (division of labor) and organizational differentiation that, in turn, results in the creation of new, and the reordering of existing, social positions (or statuses) such that a systematic alteration in moral, cognitive, and aesthetic norms occurs. That is, technological change induces a particular rate of social change, where social change is defined as a change in moral, cognitive, and aesthetic norms.[7]
4. If social order is to be maintained, a given rate of social change requires some minimum consideration of the unanticipated consequences arising from that change. The anticipation of consequences as well as an understanding of the changing order requires the

---

[5] See Edwin Mansfield, *The Economics of Technological Change* (New York: W. W. Norton, 1968), particularly Chapter II, "Technological Change and Productivity Growth," about the notion of technological change and its measurement.
[6] There is much in Fritz Machlup, *The Production and Distribution of Knowledge in the United States* (Princeton: Princeton University Press, 1962), that supports this contention; Machlup shows that in the original development of new technical knowledge, however, research within institutions of higher education plays only a small role.
[7] See Talcott Parsons, *The Social System* (Glencoe: The Free Press, 1951), Chapter XI.

THE HIGHER EDUCATION CURRICULUM 23

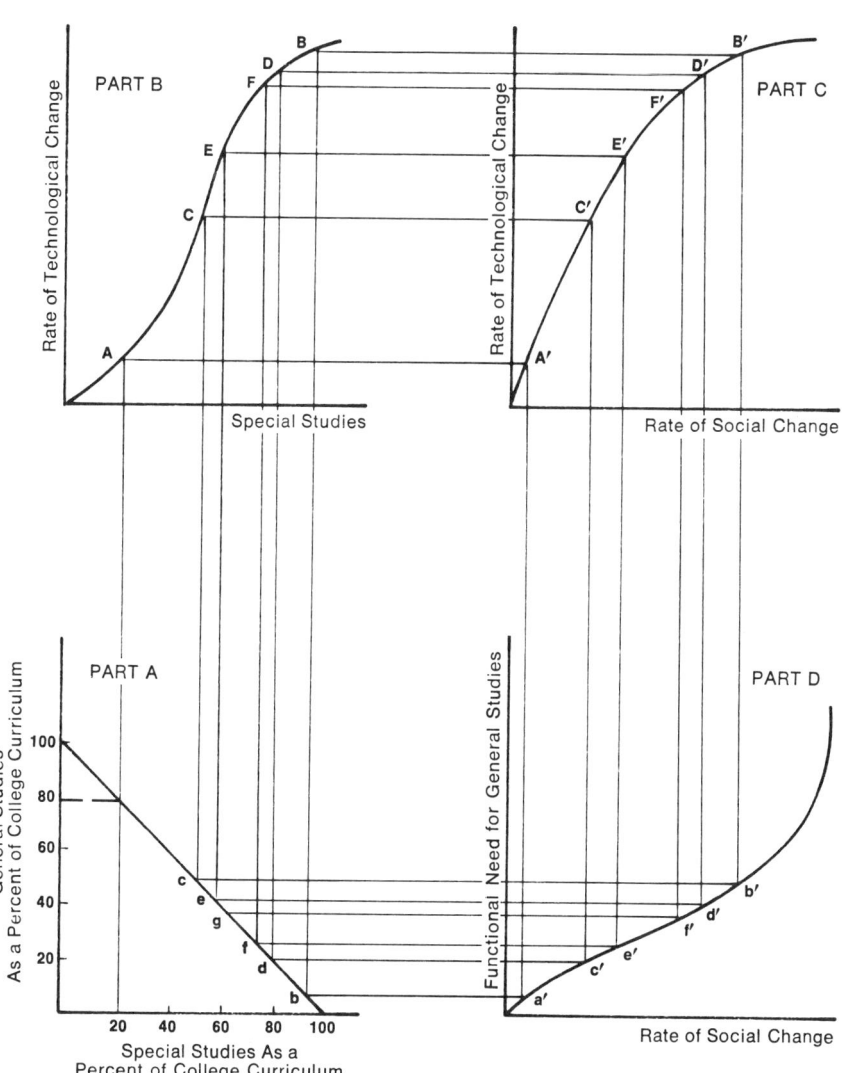

FIGURE 4. Technological Change, Social Change, and the Higher Education Curriculum

integration of methods of social and scientific investigation; thus, a given rate of social change creates a social need for research in, and the teaching of, general-integrative (or interdisciplinary) studies.

5. There is a tendency for higher education to expand through increases in academic specialization, through the subdivision of existing areas of knowledge.[8]

6. There is, on the other hand, a tendency for the higher education curriculum to respond to societal pressures for general-integrative studies through changes in the course requirements for various degrees and the development of disciplines that combine or recombine various areas of knowledge. Examples of this are ecological studies and the field of international relations.[9]

THE FUNCTIONAL RELATIONSHIPS

These six assumptions, or hypotheses, reduce to a set of four functional relationships and a balance equation, which are shown in graphic form as Parts A through D of Figure 4.

1. $RTC = f(SS)$. Rate of Technological Change is a function of Special Studies as a Percent of the College Curriculum, *ceteris paribus*. On the hypothesis that Specialized Studies cause those following major programs in such studies to produce technical refinements, whereas General Studies (*GS*) lead those majoring in *GS* programs to produce changes in the methods of approach used in the sciences and social sciences, we hypothesize that the rate of technological change is increased as a result of an increase in the number of individuals who have narrowly specialized educations, which increase is reflected in the percentage of courses in *SS* offered by institutions of higher education.

The *RTC-SS* relationship is shown in Part B of Figure 4. The *RTC* Function is non-linear, showing a period of increasing returns to increments of *SS* followed by a period of diminishing returns. The underlying hypothesis is that, as the higher education curriculum moves from *GS* toward *SS*, the new approaches produced by the *GS* students are embodied in technological advances brought about by those following an

---

[8] For an account of how Harvard expanded its subject offerings while expanding in size, see Seymour E. Harris, *The Economics of Harvard* (New York: McGraw-Hill, 1970).
[9] The reaction of U.S. engineering schools to circumstances involving both a reduction of student interest in traditional engineering areas and a reduction in the market for engineers is interesting to note. For a report of the reaction of one college, see the *Lafayette Alumnus*, January 1971, particularly the article entitled "Arts and the Engineer."

THE HIGHER EDUCATION CURRICULUM 25

SS curriculum, resulting in a period of increasing rates of technological change. As *SS* continues to increase, however, the higher degree of specialization works against the kind of communication between specialists and generalists that is essential to continued technological advance.

2. $RSC = f(RTC)$. Rate of Social Change is a function of the Rate of Technological Change, *ceteris paribus*. In society, the ways of communication, the means of production, and the major institutional forms determine the social positions both possible and needed. A social position, or status, is very much like a job, and as with any job, it cannot long survive a low level of demand or need. Any individual may occupy a number of statuses, although some individuals tend to acquire very large status sets and others acquire quite limited status sets. Each status has associated with it a number of roles, or patterned sets of mutual expectations. As statuses are elaborated in any society through the development of new modes of communication, new methods of organizing work, through new kinds of work, and through the elaboration and development of different institutional forms, new patterned sets of mutual expectations emerge. This emergence is indicated by changes in the basic norms of the society, norms governing aesthetic expression, cognitive processes (ways of organizing conceptual structures), and what is generally thought of as morality. Such changes are, by definition, the end product of what in common language is referred to as social change.

Our hypothesis concerning the relationship between Social Change and Technological Change is hardly original; many social theorists have given extended thought to this relationship and have come to conclusions not unlike ours. The way in which we have expressed the process connecting technological change with social change is an outgrowth of work done by Robert K. Merton.[10]

The *RTC-RSC* relationship is specified in Part C of Figure 4. Because society, by definition, is a complex network or web of social interconnectedness, increases in the *RTC* will be found to have ever-increasing impact on the rate of change in norms. This hypothesis is embodied in the shape of the *RSC* Curve, which indicates that successive unit increases in the *RTC* induce ever greater increases in the *RSC*. That is, the *RSC* Curve is drawn to show increasing returns to increments of *RTC* throughout the range of variation.

---

[10] Robert K. Merton, *Social Theory and Social Structure* (New York: The Free Press, 1968).

3. $FNGS = f(RSC)$. Functional Need for General Studies is a function of the Rate of Social Change, *ceteris paribus*. Here we see two uses of the term function, one sociological and one mathematical. When a sociologist speaks of a functional need, he is referring to a particular job the society needs to have performed if it is to survive and adapt. The hypothesis is that a society undergoing a change in its norms induced by a change in its range and kind of social positions induced by a change in its technological structure has a need for the kind of input General Studies produce. For example, given our situation in the United States, we have a need to better understand the position of minorities in our society, as well as a need to better understand the ecological implications of our advancing technology. In addition, we have a need to better understand the social implications of increasing urbanization. Needs are not of the same order as prerequisites. In Parsonian terms, a prerequisite is a necessary condition for the survival of the system. A need, on the other hand, is something for which there is an effective demand, something that is manifestly desirable, and something that we can usually get along without for an extended period of time. Needs unattended to often have a way of mounting in survival value, however, of becoming prerequisite to the continuance of the system.

The shape of the *FNGS* Curve in Part D of Figure 4 indicates that the induced increases in *FNGS* for unit increases in *RSC* are fairly constant until the system reaches rather high rates of social change, at which time the *FNGS* experiences an extreme rate of increase—the need becomes a prerequisite. Within the commonly experienced range of variation in the rate of social change, the society will not encounter the steeply rising portion of the *FNGS* Curve.

4. $SS = 100\% - GS$. The percent of Special Studies in the higher education curriculum is, by mathematical necessity, 100% minus the percentage of the higher education curriculum devoted to General Studies.

Part A of Figure 4 is constructed to perform the subtraction indicated in Equation 4. The line in Part A is drawn at a 45° angle between the two extreme possibilities, 100% *SS* and 100% *GS*. Thus, the line indicates all possible combinations of percentages of *SS* and *GS*.

5. $FNGS = GS$. The Functional Need for General Studies tends through the operation of the system to call into being a level of

General Studies in the higher education curriculum equal to the needed level, *ceteris paribus*. This is the balance equation in the system, and it performs the same function (job) as did the statement in the Plato model that $RFS = AFS$. In the Plato model, however, the equality was maintained as a matter of policy through the operation of an institution, a formal institution specifically designed to maintain the prerequisite equality. In the system at hand, the equality is maintained through the operation of an autonomous system and is the latent function (the unrecognized job) of various groups in the society. In economic models of the market, such as the model of price determination, the equality of quantity supplied and quantity demanded, $S = D$, is of the same autonomous kind; it is maintained or is the tendency of the system because of the operation of a set of spontaneous mutual adjustments on the part of the individuals forming the system.

The equilibrium condition is fulfilled when, across Parts D and A, there is an equality between the actual level of *GS* and the needed level of *GS*. At any moment in time, the actual level of *GS* may differ from the needed level; it is the tendency of the system to bring the two into equality, however.

THE EQUILIBRIUM SYSTEM

The system of interrelationships that spontaneously operates to bring the actual level of *GS* into accord with the needed level of *GS* can best be described as that of changing balances in an internal conflict natural to the structure of higher education. Broadly speaking, the university comprises two poles: at one pole stand those with a liberal-generalist orientation, and at the other stand the specialists. Between the poles stand the ranged ranks of those who adhere to neither extreme. The frequency distribution along the continuum between the poles is hypothesized to have but a single peak, one modal class, and it is the position of the modal class that determines university curriculum.

Universities compete for the best students, for the most prestigious faculty, and for the limited sources of external financial support. A shift in student interest, in the interests of those controlling external sources of funds, and in the interests of research-productive faculty, will, perforce, produce a shift in the position along the continuum occupied by the modal class and, hence, in the composition of the curriculum. These groups—students, financial supporters (mainly governments, foundations, and alumni), and research-productive faculty—are hypothesized to reflect the level of need for *GS* and so influence the actual level of *GS*.

The motive that makes the university responsive to the demands of these three groups is not only that of survival, but also (and primarily) prestige maximization, a point to which we shall return in Part Two.

The basic outline model is now complete. It consists of three behavioral relationships, Equations 1-3; one definitional identity, Equation 4; and one balance equation, Equation 5. Together these five statements make up a model of the dynamic equilibrium type.[11] It is dynamic because the path to a stable equilibrium is, to a degree, specified, and it is of the equilibrium (or stable equilibrium) type because any exogenous force, any parametric change, any change in any of the variables assumed constant, impounded in the *ceteris paribus* clause, will set in motion forces that will return it to a stable equilibrium position, a position in which the values of the variables of the model are such that no further change is induced from within the system.[12] The model posits that there is a combination of Higher Education Curriculum Composition (*HECC*), *RTC,* and *RSC* such that further system-induced changes in the *HECC* and in the rates of change of technology and society will not occur. Thus, the model describes a society that tends to change at a stable rate.

THE DYNAMICS OF THE MODEL

Two definitions of the term dynamic model are commonly used in the social sciences:

1. George J. Stigler defines dynamics as a "Study 'of the path by which a set of economic quantities . . . reach equilibrium within a static framework [within a framework where parametric change does not occur].' "[13]
2. Fritz Machlup defines dynamics as the "Theory of 'step-by-step adjustments . . . as sequences in time,' showing 'these movements from period to period' and the effects of different 'time sequences' depending on 'in what order [certain] steps are taken' and on the 'time intervals between the steps.' "[14]

---

[11] The best short discussion of what economists mean when they speak of dynamic systems is Fritz Machlup, "Statics and Dynamics: Kaleidoscopic Words," *The Southern Economic Journal*, XXVI (October 1959), pp. 91-110.

[12] As was the case in the Plato model, parametric changes are indicated in the diagrammatic presentation of the model by shifts in the position of the curves (functions), as well as by changes in the shape of the curves.

[13] Machlup, "Statics and Dynamics," p. 99, quoting George J. Stigler, *The Theory of Price* (New York: Macmillan, 1947), p. 26.

[14] Machlup, "Statics and Dynamics," p. 99, quoting Fritz Machlup, *International Trade and the National Income Multiplier* (Philadelphia: Blakiston, 1943), pp. 187, 188, 189.

THE HIGHER EDUCATION CURRICULUM 29

Often in economic models, such as the supply and demand model, in which it is shown how a market clearing and stable (or equilibrium) price is determined, movements prior to the establishment of equilibrium are not indicated. The curves are shifted as a reflection of some supposed change in the parameters, a new intersection of the supply and demand curve is noted, and the student is informed that this new intersection is the new combination of price and quantity such that buyers buy the amount they find it in their interest to buy at that price, sellers sell the amount that maximizes their profits to sell, and the two amounts are identical. The question as to the path followed by price and quantity movements in the time between the parametric change and the re-establishment of equilibrium is not discussed, however, and it is exactly to such a discussion that dynamics addresses itself.

Stigler's definition emphasizes the path whereby the system attains its equilibrium position. The path is particularly important in socioeconomic analysis because the variables involved are so very critical in the lives of the individuals forced along the path by the operations of the system. For example, if the path generated by the autonomous operation of the system indicates that, *ceteris paribus,* the society will have to endure a period of extremely rapid social change before a more moderate equilibrium (or stable) rate can be achieved, this knowledge may call for public action designed to override the system, causing it to find its stable position without wide variations in socially critical variables. Stigler also refers to a "static framework." This framework is parametric; that is, many very important aspects of the full system are assumed to go without change during the time in which the system follows its path to equilibrium. Technically, this holding of other things constant is accomplished by assuming that the adjustment process occurs almost instantaneously. First, we will explain the dynamics of the model using this assumption; then we will explain the model using a more realistic assumption. The results are quite different.

In his definition of dynamics, Machlup emphasizes that such models must detail the "step-by-step adjustments" of the system as it moves toward equilibrium. The Machlup approach calls for building into the model something reflecting conditions of adjustment, processes of adjustment, and estimated times of adjustment of dependent variables to changes in the values of independent variables. Thus, he speaks of the order in which steps are taken and of the time intervals between the steps. Machlup's approach to dynamics demands of the model builder a fuller, more detailed, understanding of social processes than is generally offered by models that are not socioeconomic. In short, Professor Machlup's definition requires that more hypotheses be advanced.

We now return to Figure 4. Using the instantaneous adjustment assumption, we begin with Part A and divide the Higher Education Curriculum (*HEC*) into 20% *SS* and 80% *GS*. The 20/80 combination produces a great output of basic knowledge and induces a low rate of technological change (*RTC*), indicated by Point *A* in Part B. An *RTC* of Level *A* induces a rate of social change (*RSC*) of *A'*, shown in Part C. This low value of *RSC* calls forth a low functional need for general studies (*FNGS*), indicated by Point *a'* in Part D. The university system, unchecked by a *FNGS*, follows its natural tendency to expand through subdivision and specialization, and the *HEC* instantaneously adjusts to the low *FNGS* by moving to a *HEC* composition of 95/05 (95% *SS* and 5% *GS*), indicated by Point *b* in Part A. This *HEC* composition permits the rapid exploitation of the basic knowledge produced in the previous instant and results in an extremely high *RTC*, Point *B* in Part B. Following the dynamic process to Point *B'*, Part C, we observe the induced high *RSC*, and, in Part D, the high induced level of *FNGS*, indicated by Point *b'*. Instantaneous shifts in student interest, in the direction of interest of those providing external financial support, and in faculty interest, cause the *HEC* composition to move from *b* to *c*. As the adjustment process goes through successive iterations, the system tends to settle down, successive swings in the values of the variables become less and less great until further changes in the variables all but cease, which occurs when the *HEC* composition is approximately 63% *SS* and 37% *GS*. This result may appear about right in terms of the social requirements of the nation over the long term. Given our existing stock of basic knowledge and the assumption that that stock is inadequate for the task of coping with an ecological emergency, however, it may well be that that emergency, through its influence on the position of the *FNGS* Function, Part D, will cause the system to settle on a stable *HEC* composition having a higher *GS* percentage. Each of the functions shown in Parts B, C, and D can shift to reflect changing conditions in the multitude of social facts we have consigned to the role of parameters in this model.

Let us now re-examine the dynamics of the system utilizing the more realistic assumption that the values in the model do *not* adjust instantaneously, that is, using the period analysis approach suggested in Machlup's definition of dynamics. Begin as before with an *HEC* composition of 20/80, and assume a growing university system; it is clear that the university system will be free to expand in its traditional way, through subdivision and specialization. As the *HEC* composition slowly moves toward higher levels of *SS*, and as capital investment embodies technological advancement, the *RSC* begins to pick up; this results in growing resistance to further higher education expansion through subdivision and specialization. As period after period, year after year passes,

RTC increases, but at a rate that is being slowed by a growing *FNGS*. Thus, the adjustment process can best be described as a moderately high rate of slide down along the 45° curve, Part A, which rate is being retarded by advancing levels of *FNGS*. The process may be pictured as a gradually braked slide down to and perhaps past, Point *g*, Part A; *FNGS* forces a return to Point *g* with the passage of yet more time. The period analysis approach yields a dynamic path that is free of the wide swings in values we encountered in the instantaneous adjustment reading of the model. It produces a path that is fairly direct and free of oscillations, yielding an explanation of system change that has greater analytical usefulness.

This model, as was true of Plato's model, has the somewhat unusual property of raising education, and higher education in particular, to a level of importance in accounting for societal change that is altogether at variance with most current work on the subject of social change. Everett E. Hagen's well-known work, *On the Theory of Social Change*,[15] does not even have an index listing for education, nor can one find much, if any, reference to education in many other important works on social change and social causation. Given the role of higher education in Western society and given the importance of the curricular composition of higher education both as an emergent property of the operation of societal forces and as a causal factor in the shaping of those forces, its absence from the social scientific literature on change is difficult to understand and can be only in part explained, as we are attempting to explain it, as due to the absence of a suitable method of model construction.

---

[15] Everett E. Hagen, *On the Theory of Social Change* (Homewood: The Dorsey Press, 1962).

Chapter III

LITERACY IN A MODEL OF LOW-LEVEL EQUILIBRIUM

Over the years, many social theorists have been interested in the problems posed by the developing or modernizing nations of the Third World. Using comparative analysis, economists, such as W. W. Rostow,[1] sociologists, such as Daniel Lerner,[2] anthropologists, such as Bronislaw Malinowski,[3] and social psychologists, such as David McClelland,[4] have attempted to discover the critical preconditions necessary to take off into a system of self-sustaining development and modernization.

The problems faced by Third World nations are extremely difficult to analyze and would appear to yield best to comparative analysis. The majority of the literature has been produced by economists, however, and economists tend not to make extensive use of comparative analysis.

---

[1] W. W. Rostow, *The Stages of Economic Growth* (London: The Cambridge University Press, 1960).
[2] Lerner, *The Passing of Traditional Society.*
[3] Bronislaw Malinowski, *The Dynamics of Culture Change* (New Haven: Yale University Press, 1945).
[4] David McClelland, *The Achieving Society* (Princeton: D. VanNostrand, 1961).

Rostow and writers such as Harbison and Myers,[5] and Adelman and Morris,[6] are clear exceptions. As a result of the disciplinary division of method, we have many very interesting and suggestive economic models of development for Third World nations, some of which include education as a factor, but relatively few of these have been formulated on the basis of insights drawn from comparative analysis. On the other hand, we have a large number of comparatively based sociological and political studies, but these, unfortunately, lack the exactness of formulation that the economist's method of model construction imposes. In this chapter, we will reformulate a portion of a comparative study done by a political scientist-sociologist, Daniel Lerner, in *The Passing of Traditional Society*.

THE LERNER ANALYSIS

Lerner's book has been analyzed by two economists, Irma Adelman and Cynthia Taft Morris, in *Society, Politics, and Economic Development:*

> Daniel Lerner is another student of transitional societies who emphasizes the individual's sense of participation as the essence of the "modern" outlook. In probing the sources of the participant society, he maintains that the essential element in the makeup of the modern man is a "psychic mobility" that enables him to identify with the new aspects of his environment and to adapt readily to them.[7]
>
> Daniel Lerner . . . sees political, economic, and social development as closely interrelated aspects of the modernization of society, the final stage of which is the evolution of fully participant democratic institutions.[8]
>
> [Daniel Lerner holds] . . . the view that in actuality urbanization is the first phase in the economic and political modernization of a nation and that until a country reaches some critical minimum extent of urbanization, substantial extentions of literacy, mass communication, and the associated capacity for industrialization are impossible.[9]

It is certainly generally accepted that literacy is an essential eco-

---

[5] Harbison and Myers, *Education, Manpower and Economic Growth*.
[6] Irma Adelman and Cynthia Taft Morris, *Society, Politics, and Economic Development* (Baltimore: The Johns Hopkins University Press, 1967).
[7] *Ibid.*, p. 50.
[8] *Ibid.*, p. 53.
[9] *Ibid.*, p. 26.

nomic asset in industrial urban occupations, facilitating the training of unskilled as well as skilled workers. In addition, it is an important modern mechanism for integrating both the social and political structures of a nation.[10]

These quotations fairly well summarize the theoretical content of Lerner's book. Literacy and urbanization are key components, which, when present in correct and critical proportion, lead to "psychic mobility," and psychic mobility is *the* critical precondition necessary to the general capacity within a people to adapt to new and modern ways of social organization. Thus, from a model builder's point of view, the task is clear: construct a model that demonstrates the functional interrelationships between literacy and urbanization.

Inasmuch as our formalization of Lerner's work will yield a slightly different understanding of the relationship between literacy and urbanization from the one that Lerner presents, we will present Lerner's position in his own words:

> Sheer density of population, without countervailing urbanization, operates . . . as an anti-literacy force in most societies. Education is cheaper when pupils live close together and hence, other things being equal, density should be associated with greater literacy. But, without urbanization, other things are *not* equal—i.e., the production, distribution, and consumption of wealth are much lower. This has a direct depressing effect on all public services, notably free public education. Dense non-urban societies, where national income is relatively small, tend to maintain relatively fewer schools by public funds; also, since per capita income is lower and less widely distributed, fewer individuals can afford to attend school. . . . in populous societies urbanization is the intervening variable and is crucial for the take-off toward increasing literacy. Only when dense populations show a significant rate of urbanization do literacy rates begin to rise.[11]

The basic problem, then, is that of inadequate levels of urbanization. This is but another way of saying that without the productive capacity implicit in urban structures there is inadequate wealth to sustain a level of public education that will, over time, lead to yet higher levels of per capita income and, through capital accumulation, to higher levels of urbanization.

---
[10] *Ibid.*, p. 36.
[11] Lerner, *The Passing of Traditional Society*, pp. 65-66.

A SOCIOECONOMIC MODEL OF THE LERNER ANALYSIS

Economists, at least since the time of Keynes, have been accustomed to analyzing certain stationary states in terms of models of low-level equilibrium. When faced with a situation in which repeated efforts to increase the level of employment (or, in this case, urbanization) fail, the model builder attempts to capture through functional interrelationships the system responsible for maintaining the undesired condition. The notion is that some powerful and socially fundamental set of relationships is at work overcoming all efforts to dislodge the system from its low-level position; this position is always reattained regardless of temporary dislodging. Destruction of the low-level equilibrium system, once the form of the system is understood, is the task of the development planners, and the term applied to the strategy designed to destroy the system is usually that of Critical Minimum Effort.[12]

Our model of low-level equilibrium based upon Lerner's understanding of developmental processes is presented in Figure 5. The model employs the notions of supply and demand, and is a direct outgrowth of this statement by Lerner:

> . . . increases in urbanization tend in every society to multiply national increases in literacy and media participation. By drawing people from their rural communities, cities create the *demand* for impersonal communication. By promoting literacy and media, cities *supply* this demand.[13]

Figure 5 has two curves, *DD* and *SS*. Curve *DD*, Lerner's Demand Curve, shows the percentage of literacy necessary (functionally required) in a particular country, *ceteris paribus*, to sustain any degree of urbanization. The Demand Function is drawn to indicate, for different percentages of the population living under urban conditions, the minimum percentage of literacy required to sustain those different percentages of urbanization. Within the *ceteris paribus* condition are such things as the natural resources of the country, its geography, its climate, its international trade opportunities, the inflow of capital, the availability of local and foreign entrepreneurs, etc. The curve illustrates a situation in which the country is badly positioned; that is, it takes a very high percentage of literacy to sustain a relatively low level of urbanization. The *DD* Curve will become

---

[12] For an excellent discussion of the Critical Minimum Effort thesis and other matters related to growth and development in Third World nations, see Harvey Leibenstein, *Economic Backwardness and Economic Growth* (New York: John Wiley & Sons, Inc., 1963).

[13] Lerner, *The Passing of Traditional Society*, p. 61 (emphasis added).

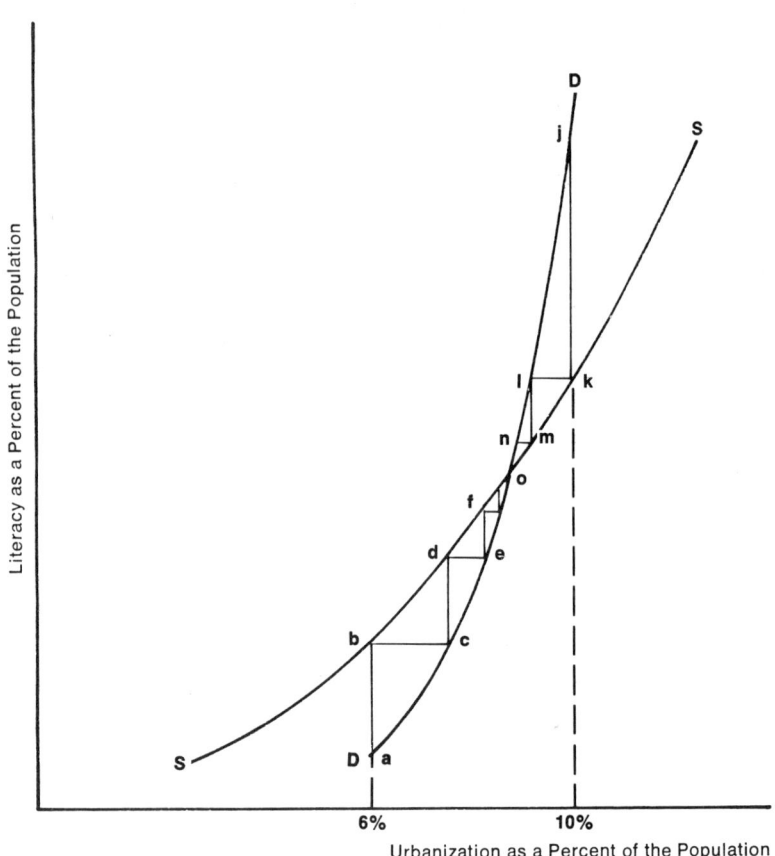

FIGURE 5. A Low-Level Equilibrium Model of the Urbanization Process

less steep, *ceteris paribus,* as outside human and material capital become available either because of enhanced export opportunities or because of foreign aid.

The Supply Curve, *SS,* shows, *ceteris paribus,* the availability of literate persons as a percent of the population at each level (percentage) of urbanization. According to Lerner, as urbanization increases, the cities project an image of the new that is received by those with empathic capacity residing in rural situations. These people, through a process commonly known as anticipatory socialization, facilitated by their literacy, prepare for and then are drawn to the city, thus supplying what urbanization requires, additional city inhabitants holding modern sets of values and orientations. In addition, it is assumed that these new moderns will begin to demand schooling for their children, a demand that prompts their entrance into the opinion-forming category as well as into the ranks of those who are political participants. Given the reaction of the government, the availability of funds, the availability of teachers, etc. (all things held equal), the system responds to an increase in urbanization, and a certain increase in quantity supplied becomes available after a given period of time. Additional supply facilitates an increase in urbanization, which, in turn, creates demand, and increases in quantity demanded cause increases in conditions determining quantity supplied. The basic quantities supplied and demanded in interaction one with the other are limited by the parameters of the society, however, and until parametric change occurs, the stable equilibrium position may well be one of low-level equilibrium.

The 6% level of urbanization requires (demands) a percentage of literacy indicated by Point a on the DD Curve in Figure 5. That is, a 6% level of urbanization cannot be sustained if the level of national literacy is below a percent. Given the dynamics of the system, a 6% level of urbanization induces or causes the availability of b percent of literates, which makes possible the expansion of urbanization to the c level. After a period of time, the c level of urbanization, the maximum level possible given the demands of urbanization and the b or c level of literacy, causes the supply of literates to increase to the percentage indicated by Point d on the SS Curve. Successive increases in urbanization have diminishing capacity, *ceteris paribus,* to induce increases in quantity supplied. Thus, the system comes to rest at the intersection of the Supply and Demand Curves.

Let us now consider the dynamics of the system to the right of the intersection of the curves. Attaining a position to the right may be the object of some external institution, such as the World Bank and the Bank's development planners. Suppose that the Bank mounts a large effort in the country and, as a result of this effort, urbanization is raised to the 10% level. At the termination of the project, will the country be able to sustain its 10% level of urbanization, or will many people be forced to return to their villages?

Assuming that the foreign presence changed none of the basic parametric forces in the society, Figure 5 indicates that the 10% level will not be sustained. At the 10% level, a level selected because, as Lerner states it, "about 10% of the population must be urbanized before the 'take-off' occurs,"[14] the Demand for literates is at the j level, but the system can Supply only k percent. Since k is only adequate to sustain

---

[14] *Ibid.,* p. 61.

an l level of urbanization, urbanization will fall to the l level. But, when urbanization is at the l level, the combination of the amount of urban-induced spending on schools and the impact of this level of urbanization on the countryside, etc., causes the quantity supplied to fall to the m level, and so on until the low-level equilibrium position is once again attained.

Inasmuch as a downward shift of the DD Curve may prove quite difficult, the policy implications of this model are clear: change those parameters controlling conditions of supply, and shift the Supply Curve upward. Drawing upon a real world example, the Shah of Iran, through implementing land reform and establishing a Teacher Corps as a subsector of the armed forces of that country, as well as investing a larger proportion of oil revenues in social infrastructure, may be seen as acting to shift Iran's SS Curve upward.

METHODOLOGICAL CONSIDERATIONS

The beginning student of socioeconomic model building may well wonder why the Lerner model is so different in construction technique from that employed in the previous two models. The decision about the form a model takes must, when first approximations are sought, follow the principle of Ockham's Razor, i.e., that variables (entities or essences) must not be increased beyond what is necessary. In model construction, one attempts to represent the essence of the system with as few variables as possible. In the case at hand, that happened to be two variables; thus, both of the functional relationships relating these two variables could be shown in one graph.

Because the application of Ockham's Razor to the graphic technique used in the Lerner model may have made it appear that something essentially different was involved in the analytical technique employed, we will reformulate the Lerner model using exactly the same procedure as in the previous two models. We begin with a symbolic statement of the functional relationships involved:

1. $U=f(L)$. The percentage of the population that is urbanized is, in the early stages of development, a function of the percentage of the population that is literate, *ceteris paribus*. This is a formal statement of the relationship graphically displayed as the DD Curve in Figure 5. Looked at from the demand perspective, it indicates the level of literacy functionally prerequisite to, or demanded by, any level of urbanization.
2. $L=f(U)$. The percentage of the population that is literate is a function of the level of urbanization, *ceteris paribus*. This states

in formal notation the relationship graphically illustrated by the *SS* Curve. From the supply perspective, it indicates the level of literacy that will tend to be supplied on account of the educational efforts that were induced by the existence of some level of urbanization in combination with the autonomous socialization processes inducing literacy, processes that are one aspect of the emergent properties of increasing urbanization.
3. *ILL=RLL*. This is the balance equation; it states that the system tends to produce a condition in which the Induced Level of Literacy (*ILL*) is equal to the Required Level of Literacy (*RLL*). This condition exists at the point where the Supply and Demand curves intersect. To the left of the intersection, where *ILL* is greater than *RLL,* the dynamic process results in increases in both percent of literacy and percent of urbanization. To the right of the intersection, where *ILL* is less than *RLL,* both percent of literacy and percent of urbanization will fall.

Figure 6 is a graphic reformulation of the model shown in Figure 5. With one exception—the basic shape of the *DD* Curve [15]—this model is exactly the same as the one in Figure 5; that is, it reaches the same conclusion and it does so utilizing the same dynamic process. The model in Figure 6, however, appears in a form with which the reader is now familiar.

Parts B and D of Figure 6 are void of theoretical content and simply perform the function of taking values determined in either Part A or Part C and projecting them through a 90° turn, a task that is performed by the 45° angles drawn in Parts B and D.

Beginning with Point *a* in Part A and following the path in a clockwise direction, we note that *a* percent Literacy causes (permits) the percent of Urbanization to achieve the level indicated by Point *1* on the *DD* Curve. This level of Urbanization induces a supply of literates indicated by Point *3* on Curve *SS,* Part C, which, in turn, leads to a level of Urbanization indicated by Point *5* on Curve *DD,* Part A. With each iteration of the dynamic process, the increase in Urbanization grows smaller. Curve *DD* has been superimposed on Part C and is labeled Curve *D'D'*. The intersection of the *D'D'* and *SS* Curves is, as before, the equilibrium position. If we begin the process at Point *b* in Part A

---

[15] The *DD* Curve in Figure 5 indicates that the required level of literacy increases by ever greater increments as the percentage of the population that is urbanized increases. Graphically this is indicated by the *DD* Curve's slope becoming steeper as percent of urbanization increases. By way of contrast, in Figure 6 we show a *DD* Curve in which the increments to percent of literacy for increments to percent of urbanization diminish. This is indicated by the *DD* Curve's becoming less steep as percent of urbanization increases. Both hypotheses are subject to statistical verification.

40   SOCIOECONOMIC METHODS

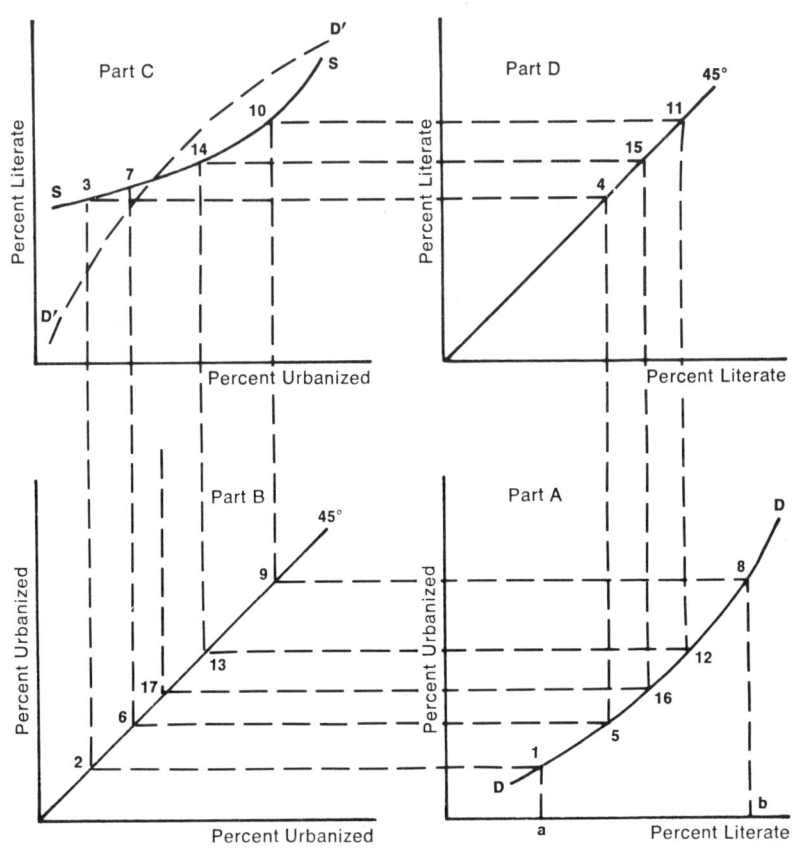

FIGURE 6. A Model of Low-Level Equilibrium

and follow the dynamic process to its conclusion, the same result will be obtained as was obtained with values of U to the right of the intersection in Figure 5; that is, the value of U will fall until $ILL = RLL$.

STABILITY CONDITIONS IN EQUILIBRIUM MODELS

We have presented a model of stable low-level equilibrium. This model could be converted into one of high-level stable equilibrium simply by shifting the SS Curve upward. An interesting technical point arises, however, when we consider what would be necessary to convert the model into one of unstable equilibrium. An unstable equilibrium is one that, if disturbed (pushed off of its equilibrium point) will, depending upon the direction of the push, either move explosively in the direction of unconstrained increase or die off by moving rapidly into the origin, unless a point of stable equilibrium is encountered prior to the origin. Such a point of unstable equilibrium would exist if Curves SS and $D'D'$ in Part C were extended to the right until they intersected. To the right of the projected intersection, the model would move explosively in the direction of 100% Literacy and 100% Urbanization; the process would come to a halt as soon as either L or U reached 100%. To the left of the projected intersection, the system would fall until it encountered the stable equilibrium point. The fact that an equilibrium point may be either stable or unstable requires that the model builder specify the stability conditions of his model. In this case, the stability condition is that the DD Curve cut the SS Curve from beneath. The DD Curve cuts the SS Curve from above at the projected intersection and therefore results in the production of an unstable equilibrium. The reader can work out the dynamics of explosive disequilibrium to the right of the unstable equilibrium point.

Part Two
MICROSOCIETAL CONSIDERATIONS

Chapter IV

A SOCIOECONOMIC MODEL OF THE DETERMINANTS OF THE CONCEPTUAL LEVEL OF THE CURRICULUM

We now begin the application of the socioeconomic method of analysis at the microsocietal level. Inasmuch as the problems we will examine are not those associated with the smallest social systems, some explanation of the prefix *micro* is in order. The discipline of economics has for some years been divided into two major parts, microeconomics and macroeconomics. Macroeconomics deals primarily with theories that aggregate large numbers of somewhat similar economic actors into single groups for the purpose of analyzing the behavior of the whole economy. The parallel with our term macrosocietal is clear. When an economist deals with the parts that compose the economy, such as the operation of the market system or some particular industry that is part of the market system, he terms the study microeconomic. Clearly, some studies are more micro than are others, but generally all studies that are not macro are termed micro. Paralleling the usage economics has established, we term microsocietal any investigation that deals with systems of interaction among formal organizations. Social systems smaller than microsocietal are, by and large, those existing within formal organizations. Studies of such systems are termed organization theoretic; some examples of this appear in Part Three below. This latter usage also parallels that of economics, although many economists do not consider organization theory a part of economics proper, mainly, it may be supposed, because such studies involve the obvious use of concepts drawn from the disciplines of sociology and social psychology.

The model we will be dealing with in this chapter does involve the use of both economic constructs and constructs built from theories developed in social psychology. Unlike most of the models we are examining, this model is not an equilibrium one. It attempts to explain an educational phenomenon associated with changing conditions of supply and demand in the market for teacher services. Given conditions of supply and demand and the institutional factors responsible for salary determination in the market for teacher services, the educational system operates to produce curricular change as a function of changes in the given conditions.

THE FUNCTIONAL RELATIONSHIPS AND THE MODEL

The functional relationships of the model are as follows:

1. $S_{LM}=f(P)$. The number of teachers supplied to a given school district, to a given local market (LM), is a function of price (or wage), *ceteris paribus*. Within the *ceteris paribus* condition are such things as the image of the school district in the minds of prospective teachers, the district's recruitment effort, the output of teachers from regional colleges and universities, and the image and recruiting efforts of competing school districts. The Supply Curve, Curve S_{LM}, is shown in Part A, Figure 7.
2. $D_{LM}=f(P)$. The number of new teachers demanded by a given school district is a function of the institutionally determined wage (or price), *ceteris paribus*. Within the *ceteris paribus* condition are such things as the income of the school district (which is influenced by local economic conditions, state and federal aid, etc.), projected enrollment, teacher turnover and retirement, and existing plant and equipment. The Demand Curve, Curve D_{LM}, is shown in Part A, Figure 7.

The intersection of the Supply and Demand Curves has nothing whatsoever to do with the determination of the wage that is offered. If the school district was but one small part of a national or regional market

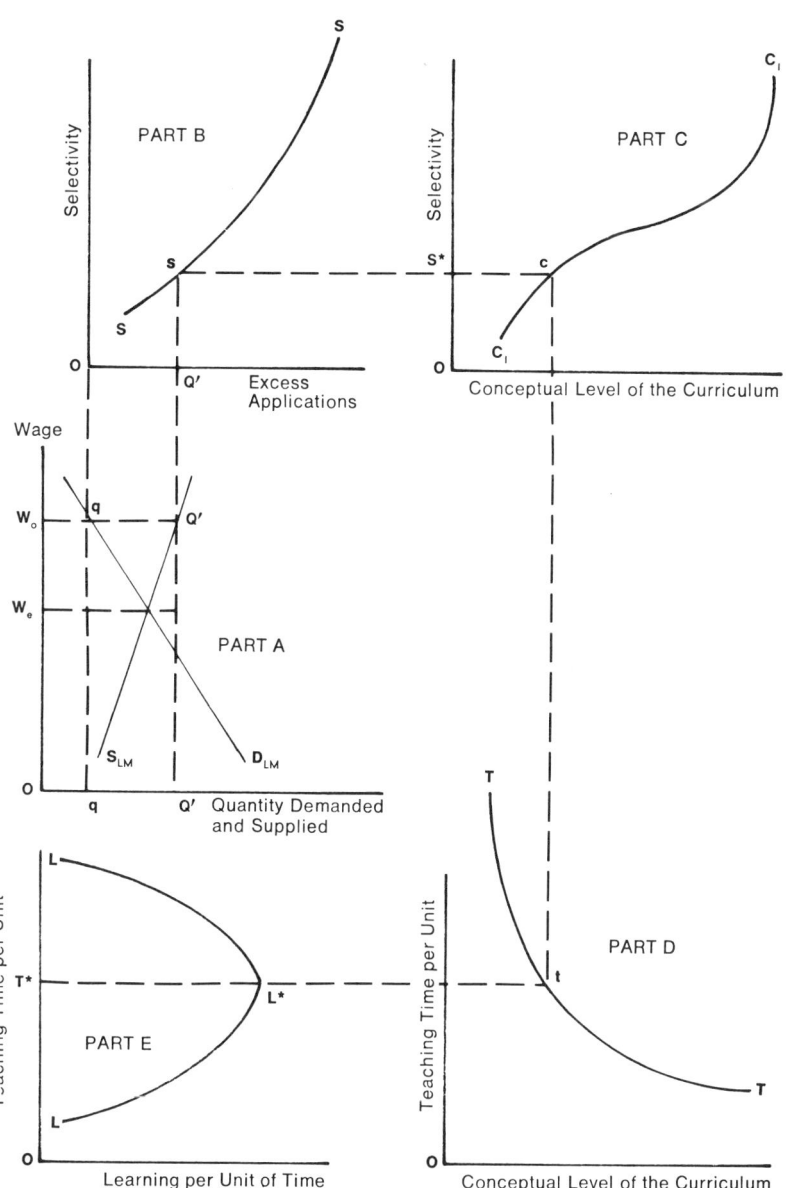

FIGURE 7. A Model of the Determinants of Optimal Teacher Salary

for teachers, its wage offering would be determined by the operation of the national (or regional) market and would tend to be a market clearing, or equilibrium, wage. If Part A were a representation of the national conditions of Supply and Demand, which it is not, and if all teachers were very much alike, then the forces of supply and demand would tend to move the wage to that indicated by W_e in Part A of Figure 7.

Our hypothesis is that the market for teacher services is very much a local affair. This hypothesis is built on several considerations, one of the most important being that teachers have a strong preference for positions close to their established homes. The fact that a large percentage of elementary and secondary school teachers are women makes it difficult to draw conclusions concerning their rates of geographic mobility; according to a 1967 study on the subject of geographic mobility among professional workers, however, only nine of 33 professional occupations had lower distant migration percentages than did elementary and secondary school teachers. During the five-year period 1955-1960, 26% of elementary and secondary school teachers moved within the same county, 10% moved within the same state, and 5% moved to a bordering state. Only 8% of elementary and secondary teachers made distant moves, and 46% made no move at all.[1] Given the low migration rates for elementary and secondary teachers, we may infer that there is a preference for locality that results in a local market. Given the nonmarket, or market insensitive, means by which teacher salaries in public schools are determined, the conditions exist to make Part A of Figure 7 an adequate representation of local market conditions.

Part A of Figure 7 illustrates a situation in which the Institutional Wage has been set at W_o. The quantity of teachers demanded at W_o is q, and the quantity of applicants is Q', which results in qQ' excess applications; this quantity of excess applications appears on the Excess Applications axis of Part B as Q'.

3. $S=f(EA)$. Selectivity is a function of the number of Excess Applications, *ceteris paribus*. Teachers vary greatly in their personal characteristics and in their professional preparation; thus, the greater the number of Excess Applications (EA), the more Selective can the school district be in its choice of teaching staff. The degree of selectively that can in practice be exercised is dependent upon the Quality Distribution of the applicants, however, and that Quality Distribution is being held constant under the *ceteris paribus* condition.

---

[1] Jack Ladinsky, "Occupational Determinants of Geographic Mobility Among Professional Workers," *American Sociological Review, 32* (April 1967), Table 1, Percentage of Mobile Professional, Technical and Kindred Workers, 1955 to 1960, by Detailed Occupation for the United States, Ranked by Migration Rate, p. 256.

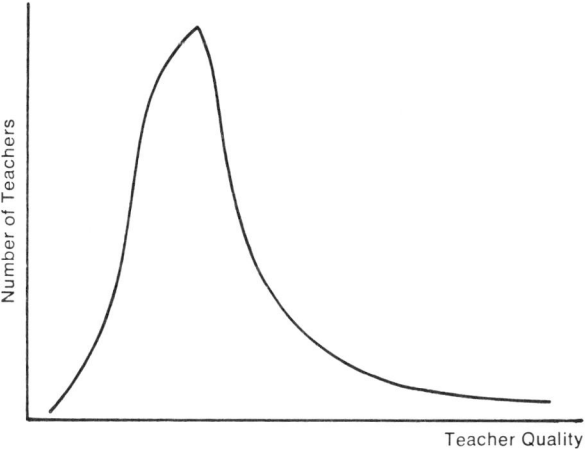

FIGURE 8. Teacher Quality Frequency Distribution

Part B is the graphic specification of Equation 3. It shows that Selectivity is an increasing function of the number of Excess Applications. The frequency distribution of teachers, ranked by quality,[2] determines the shape and position of the Selectivity Function, Curve SS. A hypothetical frequency distribution, a Quality Distribution of teachers currently in the market, is shown in Figure 8. Important factors affecting the area under the frequency distribution are the economic conditions of the locality, the regional capacity for producing teachers, and the overall level of regional college enrollment. Some of the more important factors influencing the shape of the distribution are the quality of local teacher education programs, state certification requirements, and the status system controlling recruitment to public school teaching.[3]

It may be supposed, for example, that the area under the curve, which gives the total number of teachers in the market at Institutional Wage W_o, might be reduced and its shape made more normal (less skewed) by changes in state certification requirements that de-emphasized methods courses and emphasized preparation in the subject(s) to be taught. Such changes might have the effect of changing the quality composition of those making up the Excess Applications and, therefore, would have

---

[2] Since the term *quality* is so difficult to define as applied to teachers, a discussion of teacher quality measurement will not be given in this chapter. Chapter VII contains a fuller discussion of what we mean by *quality*.
[3] On the characteristics of students entering teacher-training programs, see George C. Stern, "Student Ecology and the College Environment," *Research in Higher Education* (Princeton: College Entrance Examination Board, 1965), pp. 35-52.

the effect of shifting the *SS* Curve in Part B upward and increasing its steepness. Such changes would also affect the S_{LM} Curve, shifting it to the left. Under the conditions specified, Part B indicates that OQ' Excess Applications will be received at the Institutional Wage W_o, resulting in a Selectivity Level of s.

4. $CLC = f(S)$. The Conceptual Level of the Curriculum is a function of the Selectivity Level, *ceteris paribus*. Greater intelligence combined with superior preparation are the indicators of achieved increases in Selectivity. Teachers having both high intelligence and superior preparation are able to communicate with their students on a higher conceptual plane than are average teachers.

Perhaps the most important (and most difficult to measure) aspect of any curriculum is its conceptual level. The higher-quality teacher has, by definition, both the ability and the inclination to present Units of Knowledge at a high level of conceptualization, emphasizing the operation of general principles and the broader implications of specific analytical techniques. Such teachers have an orientation toward method rather than toward the facts. In other words, the high-quality teacher communicates to his students both a cognitive style and a set of concepts as well as the facts to be ordered through the action of the concepts and cognitive style. An interesting statement on this matter as it bears on the Conceptual Level of the Curriculum is found in Harvey *et al:*

> We assume that an individual interacts with his environment by breaking it down and organizing it into meaningful patterns congruent with his own needs [which the teacher is acting to shape] and psychological make-up. As a result of this interchange, perceptual and behavioral constancies develop, which stem from the individual's standardized evaluative predilections toward differential aspects of his external world. We will refer to such evaluative tendencies as concepts. In serving as modes of relatedness or connecting ties between the individual and his environment, concepts thus provide the basis for understanding the joint effect of situational and dispositional factors.[4]

Thus, we argue that the curriculum of one school may be quite usefully distinguished from that of another on the basis of the Effective Curriculum's efficiency in aiding the child to develop subject-object ties. To

---

[4] O. J. Harvey, D. E. Hunt, and Harold M. Schroder, *Conceptual Systems and Personality Organization* (New York: John Wiley & Sons, 1961), p. 1.

put the matter most directly, it matters less, within limits, what is taught than how it is taught, and the how is directly connected with the Conceptual Level of the Curriculum. To use a humble example, the new math was an effort to raise the conceptual level at which mathematics is taught to beginning students. Regardless of the instructional materials provided, however, the teacher's quality is the key factor setting the curriculum's Conceptual Level.

Part C of Figure 7 specifies the relationship between Selectivity and the Conceptual Level of the Curriculum (CLC). The shape of the CLC Function, Curve C_1C_1, reflects the assumption that as S increases from low levels of Selectivity there are increasing returns to CLC; due to the difficulty of accomplishing continued increases in the CLC, however, a point is reached after which increments to S produce positive but diminishing returns to CLC. The CLC accomplished by the s level of Selectivity, S^* on the vertical axis of Part C, is c, as indicated on the C_1C_1 Curve of Part C.

5. $TTU = f(CLC)$. Teaching Time per Unit of Knowledge is a function of the Conceptual Level of the Curriculum, *ceteris paribus*. In teaching, the essence of the matter is critical. In communicating the essential principles embodied in any unit of knowledge, the high-quality teacher will, through the use of a conceptual approach, compress the presentation. Saving time is not the object of teaching at high levels of conceptualization, but it is, nonetheless, the result.

If one were to take any standard academic unit and count the number of class meetings it took a teacher to present the unit, one would find, according to our hypothesis, that those teachers operating at high conceptual levels would do the job in less time. The Time Function, Curve TT in Part D of Figure 7, indicates that as CLC increases, TTU falls. The shape of the Time Function indicates that there are diminishing returns to CLC in terms of reductions in TTU along the length of the TT Curve and that the rate of diminution increases as CLC increases. One might term the hypothesis embodied in the shape of the TT Curve the Law of Increasing Resistance to Increased Compression. An example of compression achieved through the application of high levels of conceptualization is, in addition to model construction, poetry (hence the expression poetic compression). Point t on Curve TT, Part D, indicates the Teaching Time per Unit of Knowledge resulting from the c level of CLC.

6. $LUT = f(TTU)$. Learning per Unit of Time is a function of

Teaching Time per Unit of Knowledge, *ceteris paribus*. Inasmuch as TTU is determined by CLC, we could also state that $LUT = f(CLC)$; because it is desirable to state our functional relationships in causal order, or sequence, however, Equation 6 is the preferred form. Thus, any TTU implies a combination of both TTU and CLC, a combination that is functionally determined.

The Learning Function, Curve LL in Part E of Figure 7, indicates the character of the functional relationship stated in Equation 6. The hypothesis embodied in the shape of the LL Curve is that, *ceteris paribus*, there is an optimal TTU (or combination of TTU and CLC) such that at that optimal TTU, learning per unit of time is maximized. The hypothesis is that LUT rises to some maximum as TTU falls and then, as TTU continues to fall, LUT also falls. The shape of the LL Curve will, accordingly, always have a point of maximum LUT; the value of TTU at which this peak occurs and the value of LUT at the peak will, however, vary as a function of the characteristics of the students being taught. Thus, within the *ceteris paribus* condition underlying the exact shape and position of the LL Curve is the factor of student ability.

The hypothesis we are advancing maintains that it is a combination of both CLC and TTU, or pace of teaching and learning, that is important in determining the amount of learning acquired by students within a given period of time. Combinations involving low levels of conceptual content and low levels of pace will result in low acquisition rates per unit of time. At the other extreme, combinations of high CLC and high pace will also result in low acquisition rates per unit of time. Between the extremes there is an optimum combination, indicated by Point L^* on Curve LL.

Considering the model in its entirety, Institutional Wage W_o causes, given conditions of supply and demand, a level OQ' of Excess Applications. This OQ' level results in a level of Selectivity s, which produces a CLC of c. The c level of CLC causes a TTU of t, which is exactly the TTU necessary to maximize the LUT, given the available students. Thus, W_o is the optimal wage. A wage in excess of W_o will produce a combination of CLC and TTU in excess of what will maximize student learning; the reverse is true for levels of Institutional Wage below W_o.

Although a teaching staff capable of producing a combination of CLC and TTU in excess of the optimum may be assumed to be capable of adjusting to their students' ability level and thus producing the CLC and TTU combination that maximizes learning, W_o is, nonetheless, the optimal wage because it achieves the implicit system goal of learning maximization at least cost.

METHODOLOGICAL CONSIDERATIONS

The operation of a social system, particularly a microsocietal system, is very much influenced by the system's effective objective function. The objective function is a statement of the instrumentalities through which the system reaches its real objective, which may be quite different from its public, or stated, objective. In the case of the model developed in this chapter, the implicit objective was learning maximization. It must be pointed out, however, that the W_o actually set by most school systems would only be optimal in the sense developed in our model as a chance occurrence. That is, this model is not intended to imply that W_o is set with the goal in mind of maximizing learning per unit of time. If some other objective, such as harmony between school and community, is supposed, then, in certain communities, learning maximization may not be consistent with harmony. It is entirely possible, for example, that parents may see a school that provokes thought in its students as a threat to community and home stability. A school system attempting to maximize harmony might find it instrumental to that goal to maintain its *CLC* at a rather low level, in which case the Selectivity Function would rise to the level consistent with the desired low *CLC* and then become horizontal. Such a curve would indicate that, regardless of the number of applications in excess of the number of teachers to be employed, the school district would not select the best, but would, rather, select those capable of maintaining the low *CLC*. In examining such a situation, the model developed in this chapter is really not adequate. As the following chapter will show, in the case of microsocietal systems, the model must be designed around the effective objective.

Chapter V

FUNCTIONAL PREREQUISITES IN AN EQUILIBRIUM MODEL OF THE UNITED STATES SYSTEM OF HIGHER EDUCATION

The approach used in constructing the model in this chapter requires the use of a method not heretofore used in our work, that of objective function specification. Before beginning our analysis, therefore, we will discuss this new method.

Economists, faced with the problem of building a model of the operations of a market economy, had to develop a method for dealing with the great variety of firms composing a real-world market economy. Their collective decision, one determined by the operation of the laws of scientific inquiry in conjunction with the social organization of the discipline, was, essentially, to apply the method of objective function specification to the analysis of both consumer and firm behavior. This method assumes that both firms and consumers are rational actors, exhibiting behavior consistent with the maximization of a single primary objective, such as Level of Satisfaction or Utility. The consumer, given his tastes and preferences, his income, and the prices of the things he is interested in buying, is seen as spending his money in such a way as to maximize his satisfaction or utility. The business firm is seen as maximizing its Level of Satisfaction through maximizing the instrumental goal of Profit; that is, Profit is the way to utility maximization for the firm.

Given this approach to the demand and supply sides of the market, all that remained to be done was to develop a model of the representative firm to illustrate how, in general, profits are maximized, and a model of the representative consumer to illustrate how utility is maximized. Then, by placing the two together, the dynamics of their spontaneous mutual interaction could be pieced together to result in a model of the whole system. The principle construct underlying all models of spontaneous mutual interaction is that of Tendency to Equilibrium—given stability in the model's parameters, a set of values exists for the model's variables such that further changes in the values of these variables will not occur.

Once the dynamics of the system of spontaneous mutual interaction have been determined and the general equilibrium position established, it only remained for economists to determine the human implications of the operation of the market system. In working out these implications, economists applied a standard by which to judge the desirability of a state of general economic equilibrium and set about to determine whether the market system conduces to the general welfare. Thus, welfare economics has become the overtly normative portion of the discipline charged with demonstrating the desirability of the overall operations of a market economy.

In the construction of our model, we will follow the method developed by economists in their effort to model the market economy. We will first attempt to determine the objectives that institutions of higher education (*IHE*s) seek to maximize. Given a knowledge of those objectives, it then becomes possible to model the choice behavior of the representative *IHE*. In other words, just as the assumption that firms seek to maximize profits enables economists to determine what the representative firm will do when faced with a choice situation, so a knowledge of the objectives that *IHE*s seek to maximize will enable us to determine and predict the behavior (the choices) an *IHE* will make when faced with a particular situation.

In the case of a business firm, it is fairly clear that producing at least cost those things that allow the highest percentage markup will lead to profit maximization. Knowing the objective function of the representative *IHE*, however, still leaves the investigator with the problem of determining just what is instrumental to the maximum achievement of the desired goal. Thus, we must determine those actions that contribute to, or produce, the desired outcome.

Given the objective function and a knowledge of the means for achieving the objective, a model of the representative *IHE*'s choice calculus can be constructed, but this is only one half of the work required for a total analysis of the problem. The other parts are (1) determining the system of spontaneous mutual interaction that results, including a statement of the equilibrium condition for the system as a whole, and (2) evaluating the social welfare implications of the operation of the system.

THE OBJECTIVE FUNCTION

Organizations such as business firms, hospitals, colleges, and universities may appear to hold a set of objectives among which there exists a degree of logical inconsistency, such that movement toward one objective necessitates movement away from another. Thus, the organization may be conceived of as attempting to achieve some optimal balance among its many goals, a balance directed by some overarching criterion that serves to rank the goals, creating a hierarchy of objectives.

The objective function approach to the study of organizational behavior for the purpose of model construction denies the usefulness of the multiple objective approach, holding that, although descriptive, it lacks analytical power. The only valid test of any method is, of course, the results it produces. A method capable of generating models that produce explanations of past actions and predictions of general tendencies for any specified change in parametric conditions is one capable of being tested. The single objective approach, as applied in economic analysis, has produced models that have been highly successful in explaining selected aspects of the operations of a market economy. The multiple objective approach, although seemingly more descriptive, has yet to yield explanations of complex causality having the predictive power of the single objective models.

From this discussion, it would seem that if one wishes to model the representative college or university, the most effective way is that of assuming a single objective, such as prestige, and then searching out the actions that produce prestige. We maintain the correctness of this position when certain circumstances obtain: (1) Large groups of colleges and/or universities are involved and nothing has to be predicted about particular *IHE*s. (2) The effects of a specified change in conditions (in parameters) are to be explained or predicted. (3) Only qualitative answers (answers about the general kind of changes induced by the parametric changes) are sought, rather than precise numerical results.

The multiple objective approach, on the other hand, is quite useful in cases where a particular business firm, hospital, or college is being

UNITED STATES SYSTEM OF HIGHER EDUCATION 57

modeled and where precise numerical results are desired. Thus, the choice of method is entirely determined by the type of questions one seeks to answer, and if the question concerns itself with microsocietal systems rather than with organization theoretic systems, the most productive approach has been demonstrated by economists to be that of creating a theoretical construct called the representative firm or representative *IHE* or what have you. Modifying slightly what one economist has said, in socioeconomic analysis as applied to higher education, the *IHE* is a postulate in a web of logical connections.[1]

The question that now arises is that of objective function specification. How does one determine the prime objective served by the actions of a given type of organization? Inasmuch as the objective function approach has not been used much beyond economics, no standard method of specification exists. Despite the lack of work on this problem, the general solution is not so difficult to frame as might appear.

Generally speaking, one cannot discover the prime objective of an organization by asking those at the top of the administrative hierarchy to name their prime objective. In the first place, the prime objective of any one organization in a set of like organizations is of little importance when the quest is for a microsocietal model of the interactions within the set. Secondly, few managers, hospital administrators, or college presidents will, in fact, conceive of their objective function as having a single prime argument. What we seek is more subtle; in attempting to construct a model of the representative *IHE* (or hospital or foundation or government agency), what we are after is a variable that expresses the most essential underlying consideration active in all organizational decisions. Most of these decisions are the result of informal processes rather than of formal processes consciously directed toward achieving a structured moment of decision. In other words, what criterion is it that guides the course of decision as the representative organization muddles through?

We may assume that a set of like organizations represents a system for socializing those within the set in such a way that, if they are to be successful, they must hold a prescribed set of values and orientations. As Gordon Tullock has expressed it,

> The head of a hierarchy . . . has, as his principal problem in organizational efficiency, arranging the structure so that his inferiors reach decisions which he would have reached if he should have

---

[1] The thoughts developed in this paragraph are drawn rather directly from Fritz Machlup's discussion of methodology in economic analysis; see "Theories of the Firm: Marginalist, Behavioral, Managerial," *American Economic Review,* 57 (March 1967), pp. 1-33.

possessed as much information about the particular situation requiring decision as they do. The sovereign [particularly in the case where the organization has units that are geographically widespread] should not attempt to centralize decision-making directly, but rather to influence his inferiors to make decisions that fit into the grand design [or objective function] of the organization, or, more simply, into his desires.[2]

Carrying Tullock a step further, we may say that a set of organizations must seek coordination not through centralization, but through inducing the component organizations to behave in expected and desired ways. Talcott Parsons refers to this need to have components behave in expected ways as pattern-maintenance:

> ... pattern-maintenance ... has a type of "product" or contribution of generalized significance throughout the total social system. This is a type of "respect" accorded as a reward for conformity with a set of values. In cases when degrees of this respect are compared to others, we might call it *prestige*. Prestige, therefore, is the "product" of successful pattern maintenance or tension management in the interest of pattern conformity; it is a *capacity* to act in such a way as to implement the relevant system of institutionalized values.[3]

Thus, in searching for the prime objective of a set of organizations, we must first determine the value or values, conformity to which yields success by comparison to the performance of other like organizations. An examination of the historical development, from a sociological perspective, of the set of like organizations will generally reveal just exactly what this value or set of values might be. In the case of private, non-sectarian higher education, as contrasted with public higher education, pattern maintenance consists in the preservation and furtherance of those values associated with the intellectual way of life, which, essentially, is what is meant by the term prestige as applied to *IHE*s.

Given that prestige is the single objective that private, non-sectarian *IHE*s are seeking to maximize, we must now determine just what actions contribute to that maximization; that is, we must now determine how prestige is produced.

---

[2] Gordon Tullock, *The Politics of Bureaucracy* (Washington: Public Affairs Press, 1965), p. 141.
[3] Talcott Parsons and Neil J. Smelser, *Economy and Society* (New York: The Free Press, 1965), p. 51.

THE PRODUCTION FUNCTION IN HIGHER EDUCATION

When economists speak of a production function, they refer to the technological relationship between productive inputs and the resulting physical outputs of a firm or an economy. In the context of higher education, a production function is a specification of the results of a social psychological process connecting the productive inputs and the resulting outputs. These outputs are (1) socialization of students into the preferred value system, (2) embodied knowledge, and (3) production of new knowledge.

When we use the term production function, we have in mind both the input-output relationship in the educational context and the wider concept of a process that produces increases in the value (or size) of the primary objective. In the case of private, non-sectarian higher education, this primary objective is prestige—pattern maintenance about intellectual values and orientations.

In the model developed in Chapter IV the implicit objective was the maximization of learning per period of time. The production function in that model indicated that learning was maximized by adjusting the conceptual level of the curriculum to that level most in accord with the characteristics of the student input into the system. These characteristics are determined, to a very large extent, by socioeconomic and cultural factors in the lives of the students. Another factor in the production relationship was the pace of presentation, as well as the conceptual level of presentation.

The essential difference between the model developed in Chapter IV and the present model is the objective function. We did not highlight the objective function approach in Chapter IV because it is not at all clear that, in public education at the primary and secondary levels, learning maximization is the essential underlying objective. In fact, it may well be that it is not, but that harmony between school and community is the prime goal. In some cases, learning maximization may produce harmony; in other cases it may not. The operations of a public primary or secondary school, or, for that matter, of a public college or university, are constrained by political forces in a way that contrives to make harmony maximization primary. Private, non-sectarian colleges and universities can and do operate on the basis of a different objective from that forced upon their public counterparts. They do attempt to take actions that produce increases in institutional prestige.

The Importance of Value Homogeneity

Because this book is devoted to the discussion of method as opposed to one primarily concerned with defending the correctness of the hypotheses advanced (although we believe that our models are constructed from sound hypotheses), we make the following statements without attempting exhaustive proof:

1. There is a set of values and orientations that can be matched with a particular task such that, if this set is held by those composing the membership of a particular organization charged with performing the task, it will be efficiently performed.
2. Some tasks require differentiation of function (division of labor) if they are to be well performed; other tasks do not. Using Durkheim's terminology, some tasks are best performed by groups having mechanical solidarity, wherein beliefs, conduct, and (adding to Durkheim) abilities are alike. Some tasks, on the other hand, are best performed by groups having organic solidarity, wherein the group is highly interdependent, where division of labor is necessary, and where differing values, orientations, and (again adding to Durkheim) abilities are desirable as a means of apportioning the different and necessary functions.
3. In small groups performing a task where division of labor is necessary, homogeneity of values and orientations is helpful, but heterogeneity in interests and abilities is essential.
4. In small groups performing a task where division of labor is not functional (where it is, in fact, dysfunctional), homogeneity of values and orientations, given that these are the correct values and orientations, as well as homogeneity of ability, is critical. Groups comprising individuals of differing abilities have a tendency to structure, even though structuring may be dysfunctional.
5. Individual performance on a given task within a group charged with the performance of that task will be higher where the values and orientations of the group match those of the individual.

The theories and methods of sociology and social psychology will serve to explain and expand as well as test these hypotheses; what we are after at this point, however, is their collective implications for the representative prestige-maximizing IHE.[4] To draw the needed implications, two more hypotheses are necessary:

6. Harmony maximizing *IHE*s have many kinds of tasks to perform; thus, specialization and division of labor are functional to their

---

[4] Consider the work of Bruce W. Tuckman, "Group Composition and Group Performance of Structured and Unstructured Tasks," *Journal of Experimental Social Psychology*, *3* (January 1967), pp. 25-40, as his findings relate to Hypotheses 3 and 4. On Hypothesis 5, see Lawrence A. Pervin, "Satisfaction and Perceived Self-Environment Similarity: A Semantic Differential Study of Student-College Interaction," *Journal of Personality*, 35 (December 1967), pp. 623-634.

UNITED STATES SYSTEM OF HIGHER EDUCATION 61

primary goal. Therefore, differences in abilities and, to some degree, differences in values and orientations are compatible with the primary goal. The representative public *IHE* must do many kinds of things if harmony is to be maximized.

7. Prestige maximizing *IHEs* have but one basic task to perform, the production of knowledge, where production includes both producing knowledge in the minds of students and producing new knowledge. The task is undifferentiated, all are learners, all are teachers, all are critics of existing thought. The community is held together by a commonality of intellectual values and orientations, by a uniformly high level of intellect; in short, their solidarity is mechanic rather than organic. When all members of the community are learners, teachers, critics, when criticism takes the form of advancing alternative formulations as well as methodological criticism, the intellectual value pattern is maintained and prestige produced.

We will now formulate two models based on these seven hypotheses: one for the representative Prestige-Maximizing (usually Private Non-Sectarian) *IHE* and one for the Harmony-Maximizing (usually public) *IHE*.

A Model of the Representative Prestige-Maximizing Institution of Higher Eduction

Figure 9 illustrates the causal relationships or associations thought to exist in the representative Prestige-Maximizing IHE. These relationships or associations are as follows:

1. Path 1 indicates that there is an attraction between Professionalized Faculty and Private Control of an *IHE*. Traditionally, in the United States, Private Control has indicated a type of *IHE* attempting to maintain intellectual values. Professionalized Faculty (a term developed by Christopher Jencks and David Riesman) are faculty who hold intellectual values and orientations.[5] Hypothesis 4 explains why the Prestige-Maximizing private, non-sectarian *IHE* attempts to attract Professionalized Faculty; Hypothesis 5 explains why Professionalized Faculty seek out the privately-controlled *IHE*.
2. Path 2 indicates that Professionalized Faculty attempt to make admissions highly selective. Highly Selective Admissions (*HSA*) is critical to the performance of the unstructured task of knowl-

[5] Christopher Jencks and David Riesman, *The Academic Revolution* (New York: Doubleday, 1968).

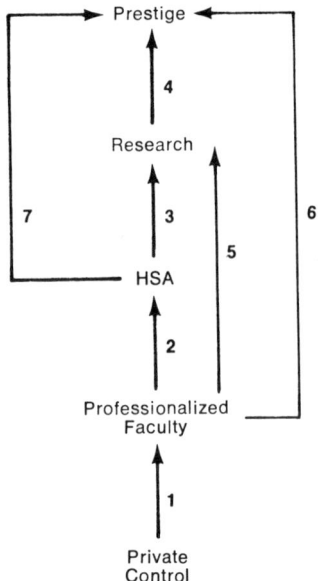

FIGURE 9. Model of Causal Relationships or Associations within the Representative Prestige-Maximizing Institution of Higher Education

edge production. The drive for *HSA* is explained by Hypotheses 5 and 7.
3. Path 3 indicates a causal relationship between *HSA* and faculty research productivity, reflecting the operation of Hypotheses 4 and 5.
4. Path 4 is almost definitional; that is, the production of research is in and of itself evidence of pattern maintenance about intellectual values.
5. Path 5 is, again, almost definitional. Professionalized Faculty have been socialized into a set of values and orientations in which the production of research is very important. The more professionalized a faculty, the higher the research output of that faculty, *ceteris paribus*. Thus, other things equal, the research productivity of a faculty of a given degree of professionalization will increase as a function of increases in admissions selectivity.
6. Path 6 indicates a functional relationship between an *IHE*'s level of Prestige and the level of Professionalization of its faculty,

which is indicated primarily by the percent of Ph.D.'s on the faculty as well as by the graduate schools where the degrees were earned.
7. Path 7 indicates that there is a functional relationship between an *IHE*'s Prestige and the level of its admissions selectivity. Having Highly Selective Admissions is an indication of the ability to attract students of high intellect, which in itself is evidence of successful pattern maintenance about intellectual values and orientations.

Taken together, the causal relationships or associations indicated by Paths 1 to 7 show how Prestige is produced and, therefore, constitute the Prestige Production Function. The statistical verification of a model such as this, a subject that takes us beyond the focus of this study, is possible. The investigator must first operationalize the variables of the model; that is, he must find real-world variables that closely represent the theoretical variables. Following operationalization, one approach is to seek to explain the variance in certain of the variables by holding them as dependent upon variations in antecedent (independent) variables. For example, if we can explain a high percentage of the variation in *HSA* by variations in the values of the variables the model indicates to be causal, then we have a fair argument for the model's actually being a correct explanation of causality. A common statistical technique for accomplishing such a test is multiple regression analysis, which seeks to determine the influence of one independent variable on the dependent variable by statistically holding the values of the other independent variables constant, thus approximating in the social area what the physical scientist more closely approximates under laboratory conditions. In addition to the direct effect of a posited independent variable on a given dependent variable, the technique may also be used to discover the paths of indirect effects—the influence on the dependent variable of a posited independent variable as that variable influences the value of some other variable that comes between, in causal sequence, the dependent variable and the independent variable being examined. Thus, Variable A may have a direct effect on Variable X, but it may also have important indirect effects because of A's influence on the size of Variables B and C, which are between A and X in causal order and themselves have direct (and possibly indirect) effects on X.

The model in Figure 9 is designed with a view toward its testability using cross-sectional data, data representing conditions at a point in time, and multiple regression analysis. It is for this reason that feedback loops are not included. One cannot easily use cross-sectional data to test a dynamic process within a model; models such as the one we are dealing with cannot therefore be of the equilibrium type. Such models can be quite useful in the early stages of theory construction, however, even when the object is the identification of a dynamic process within an equilibrium framework, a point we hope to be able to demonstrate later in this chapter.

One last point remains to be discussed before turning to the development of a model of the Harmony-Maximizing *IHE,* and that concerns the matter of whether a good statistical test of the model can be taken as a step in the verification of the hypotheses underlying the construction of the causal sequence illustrated by the path diagram. Our approach to the construction of the model in Figure 9 was first sociohistorical. The development of prestige *IHE*s was examined over time and the likely causal sequence hypothesized. The original conception was one of a dynamic process of development, one that attempted to show the feedback loops as they operated to cause certain *IHE*s to grow in prestige over time. For the purposes of statistical testing, these feedback loops were eliminated. Taking the simplified model, the hypotheses implicit in each path were stated and the social psychology literature searched for articles testing the same (or very nearly the same) hypotheses. Finding a number of supporting articles constituted a type of test of the model in and of itself. Finding that a multiple regression test of the model produced encouraging results was yet another step in model verification. If the investigator cannot conceive of alternative hypotheses to explain the paths of his model, it would seem fair to take strong statistical results on the model as inferring the essential correctness of the social psychological hypotheses.[6]

A Model of the Representative Harmony-Maximizing Institution of Higher Education

Applying the objective function approach to the task of analyzing the behavior of a set of like organizations requires that the investigator first

---

[6] One of the greatest problems facing the beginning model builder is that, in attempting to polish his method of approach, he must depend upon the insights into method he can gain from reading published studies, and, as was the case with this model, the development of the logic shown the reader is not that followed by the investigator. The reader is shown a cleaned-up version, one attempting to illustrate the orderly application of scientific method. As most scientists will agree, however, there is nothing orderly about the creative process. One has, or thinks he has, an insight into some physical or social process. Through the application of method, insights are refined, tested, and communicated, and it may not be too much to say that many valuable insights have been lost due to the observer's not having access to a suitable method. The purpose of this study is the development of a new method, one building on old methods, one capable of expressing in a disciplined way insights that may now be lost or inadequately framed because they deal with social processes that fall between the existing social scientific fields.

UNITED STATES SYSTEM OF HIGHER EDUCATION

identify the prime objective and then search out the means whereby the representative organization will produce the desired end. When the desired end is Prestige, the means of production will differ greatly from cases when the desired end is Harmony. As indicated by Hypothesis 7, the basic form of organization differs because Harmony requires division of academic labor, whereas Prestige is produced by mechanic solidarity. In addition, the two types of *IHE*s differ in the types of rewards the participants find meaningful. Our hypothesis on the matter of rewards is as follows:

8. Professionalized faculty, almost as a matter of definition, receive their principal satisfactions from professional recognition. Their reference group is their fellows in the discipline. Recognition comes as a product of publication. Non-professionalized faculty, on the other hand, depend upon their status in the local hierarchy for their primary psychic rewards, making conformity to the desires of superiors an important part of the means whereby upward movements in the hierarchy, and the rewards attaching to these upward movements, are obtained.

Hypotheses 6 and 8 taken together lead to the conclusion that the Harmony-Maximizing *IHE* will be centralist and one in which the members are quite conscious of local status differentials, all of which facilitates the attainment of the primary goal.

Figure 10 illustrates the causal sequence in the production of Harmony. The causal relationships or associations illustrated by the numbered paths are as follows:

1. Path 1 indicates that the historical association between public higher education and non-intellectual values and orientations serves to attract Non-Professionalized Faculty, in part due to the operation of Hypothesis 5.
2. Path 2 postulates a causal relationship between the degree of centralization of administrative control and the extent to which the faculty comprises non-professionalized members. Implicit in Path 2 is the operation of Hypothesis 8.
3. Path 7 indicates that, by virtue of the political nexus in which public *IHE*s operate, local service is very important. Path 3 states that there is a causal connection between Centralized Control and the degree of Local Service offered. Hypotheses 6 and 8 explain Path 3.
4. Path 4 states that Local Service leads to the production of Harmony, particularly with power bases outside the *IHE*.

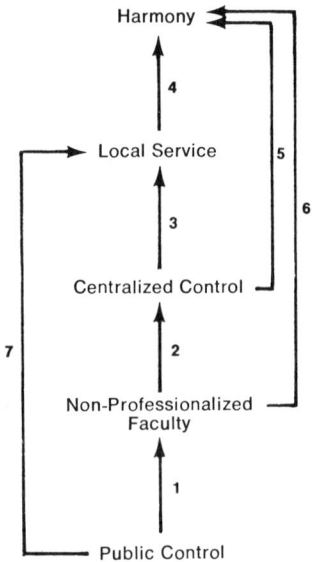

FIGURE 10. Model of Causal Relationships or Associations within the Representative Harmony-Maximizing Institution of Higher Education

5. Paths 5 and 6 indicate that Non-Professionalized Faculty in combination with the resulting Centralized Control lead to Harmony within the *IHE*. Hypotheses 6 and 8 underlie the operation of the relationships indicated by Paths 5 and 6.

Paths 4, 5, and 6 thus indicate that Harmony between the members of the Staff and Faculty of a Public *IHE* is highly important, as is Harmony between the *IHE* and the immediate community.

We have now completed our discussion of the objective function approach to model construction, a very useful technique in microsocietal analysis. What remains is to explain how this technique may be used to construct more complex models capable of predicting the behavior of a set of like organizations when these organizations are faced with a specified change in some condition exogenous (external) to the set.

A DYNAMIC MODEL OF *IHE* PRESTIGE MAXIMIZATION

During the decade of the 1960's, the Prestige-Maximizing *IHE*s in the United States were faced with a substantial change in two fundamental parameters: (1) the number of students seeking places in colleges and universities increased greatly and (2) the funds available to private and public higher education increased greatly. Given our models, what could be expected to occur in the system of Prestige-Maximizing *IHE*s? What could be expected of the Harmony-Maximizing *IHE*s?

In Figure 11 we show a model developed from the path diagram of Figure 9. The model illustrates the process whereby an *IHE* converts from Harmony Maximization to Prestige Maximization, thus increasing the number of Student Places in *IHE*s maintaining value homogeneity

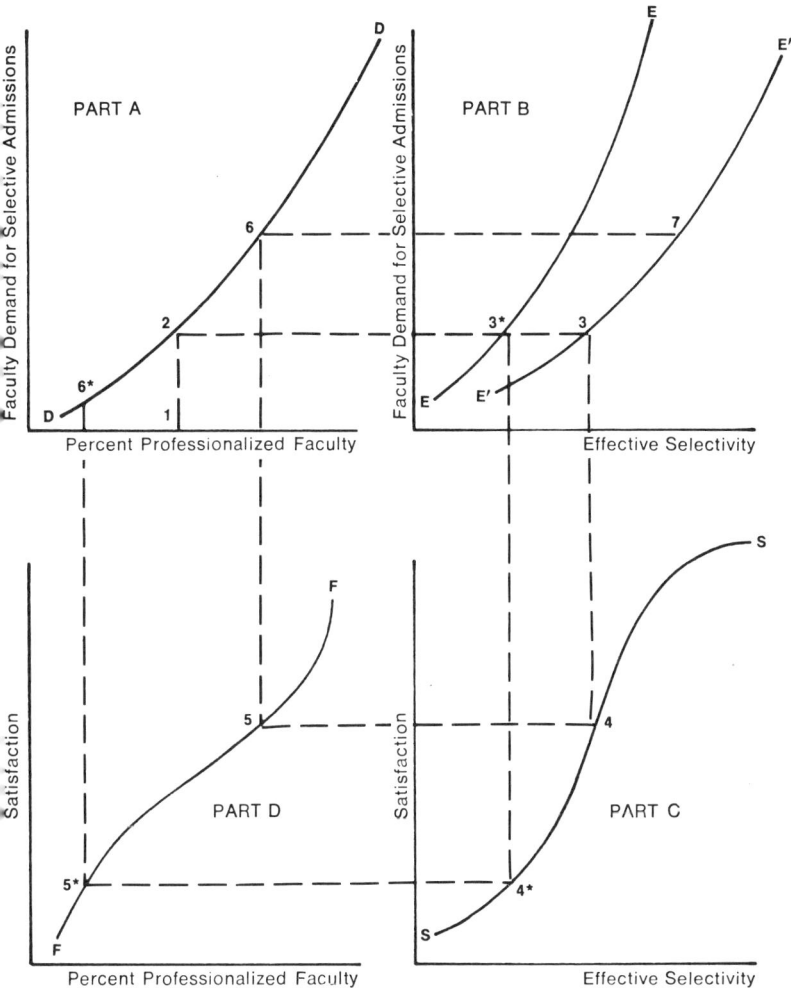

FIGURE 11. A Dynamic Model of *IHE* Prestige Maximization

about intellectual values. As we shall see, this process of conversion is an important aspect of system adjustment to changes in the flow of students into higher education. In particular, this model is an important building block in our attempt to construct a microsocietal model of the system of higher education, one that will explain the system's reaction to a large increase in the number of students seeking a higher education, as well as yielding some insight into the type of equilibrium the microsocietal system seeks to establish.

Following are the functional relationships composing the model:

1. $FDSA = f(\%PF)$. Faculty Demand for Selective Admissions is a function of the Percent of Professionalized Faculty. Curve DD in Part A of Figure 11 specifies this functional relationship. The shape of Curve DD indicates that, as $\%PF$ increases, $FDSA$ increases by ever greater increments. That is, as $\%PF$ increases the level of demand or pressure for Selective Admissions increases more than proportionately due to the fact that professional faculty support each other psychologically and structure themselves into an increasingly effective pressure group.
2. $ES = f(FDSA)$. Effective Selectivity is a function of Faculty Demand for Selective Admissions, *ceteris paribus*. Within this condition are such parameters as Type of Control (public or private) Rate of Change in Number of Students Seeking Entrance to Colleges and Universities, Established Image of the *IHE*, Scholarship Funds Available, and Attitude of Top Administration. Curves EE and $E'E'$ in Part B give two specifications of the Selectivity Function. The shape of both curves indicates that increases in $FDSA$ yield diminishing increases in ES, a relationship explained by the fact that it is increasingly difficult to achieve higher levels of student intellectualism because of the scarcity of such students Curve EE illustrates a situation in which most of the parametric conditions do not favor increases in ES; Curve $E'E'$ reflects a situation favorable to ES.

Taken together, Parts A and B of Figure 11 elaborate Paths 1, 2 and 7 of Figure 9. The hypotheses underlying Paths 1, 2, and 7 are also implicit in the joint operation of Parts A and B. In reformulating these paths, we have greatly increased the theoretical content and we have achieved an increase in generality. Although the model is being approached from the standpoint of Prestige Maximization, it may also be approached from the viewpoint of Harmony Maximization, which makes Figure 11 representative of both types of *IHEs*. That is, the model will explain why some *IHEs* remain Harmony Maximizers and

UNITED STATES SYSTEM OF HIGHER EDUCATION 69

why some are Prestige Maximizers, as well as explain the process whereby some *IHE*s convert from one objective to the other. A third functional relationship is part of the model:

3. $S = f(ES)$. Satisfaction is a function of Effective Selectivity. The Satisfaction of Professionalized Faculty depends upon their being located in an *IHE* comprising individuals having values and orientations toward intellectual pursuits. In such an environment, one of value homogeneity about intellectual values and orientations, Professionalized Faculty will be more productive in both research and teaching. The changing slope of Curve *SS*, the Satisfaction Function, in Part C reflects the hypothesis that increases in *ES* from very low levels are quite strongly felt by Professionalized Faculty. Curve *SS* indicates that the first increments to *ES* yield increasing returns to Satisfaction; a point is reached, however, where further increases to *ES* begin to yield positive, but diminishing, returns.

Part C of Figure 11 reformulates Paths 3 and 4 of Figure 9. If we were to consider Part C from the standpoint of the Satisfaction of Non-Professionalized Faculty, we would find that increases in *ES* yield Dissatisfaction. In fact, highly intellectual students may constitute a threat to the Non-Professionalized Faculty; under the parametric conditions specified, therefore, where both the number of students seeking admission to *IHE*s and the funds available to higher education are increasing, we can predict that *IHE*s controlled by Non-Professionalized Faculty and Administration will choose to expand, whereas *IHE*s controlled by Professionalized Faculty and Administration will elect to become more selective. Thus, implicit in the drive for *HSA* (or *ES*) is a constraint on size, whereas implicit in the drive for Local Service is the Need to Expand, a need growing out of the Harmony objective as well as out of the threat *ES* poses to Non-Professionalized Faculty.

There is a final functional relationship in the model:

4. $\%PF = f(S)$. Percent of Professionalized Faculty is a function of the level of Satisfaction, *ceteris paribus*. Curve *FF*, the Faculty Function, shown in Part D, is a specification of the relationship between *S* and %*PF*. Within the *ceteris paribus* condition is the ratio of total system-wide Faculty Positions Available to total Supply of Professionalized Faculty. The shape of Curve *FF* embodies the hypothesis that, under conditions where Satisfaction is high (and rising), it will be progressively easier to recruit additional Professionalized Faculty to the *IHE*. After a certain per-

centage is reached, however, increases become more difficult, partly because of the impediment of tenure and partly because staffing the higher ranks of the faculty with Professionalized Faculty means that the *IHE* must both attract and hold senior scholars, something few *IHE*s can do.

Because the Faculty Function reflects the impact of *HSA*, Research, and Prestige on Percent of Professionalized Faculty—the feedback of these factors in *%PF*—there is no equivalent path in Figure 9.

We can now examine the dynamic system formed by these four functional relationships. Beginning with Point *1* in Part A, we note that the *1* percent of *PF* causes a level of *FDSA* of *2*, and that the *2* level of *FDSA* causes either the *3** level or the *3* level of *ES*. If the *3* level, after a period of time, results from the *2* level of *FDSA*, then we can state that the parameters underlying the position of the Selectivity Function are such as to conduce *IHE* conversion to homogeneity about intellectual values. That is, given an increase in applications and in funds available, the *IHE* chooses to increase *ES* rather than size. If this is the case, we may predict that the *IHE* is private, has the Image of being a good school, has a Professionalized Administration, and has the funds necessary to compete successfully with other Prestige-Maximizing *IHE*s, in terms of scholarships offered, for the Intellectual Student. If Curve *E'E'* obtains, then the *4* level of Satisfaction will be generated and, over time, the *%PF* will increase to the *5* level, as indicated in Part D. Following this dynamic path to Points *6* and *7* in Parts A and B, we note that, because of the increase in *%PF* and in *ES*, there is, implicitly, an increase in Value Homogeneity about Intellectual Values and Orientations, thereby increasing institutional Prestige, confirming the Prestige-Maximizing objective. If Curve *EE* is the operational Selectivity Function, however, then the *3** level of Selectivity is generated by the *2* level of *FDSA*. This causes the level of Satisfaction to reach the *4** level, which is consistent with maintaining a *5** level of *%PF*, which is less than that with which the *IHE* started. Given this dynamic path, it is possible to predict that the *IHE* is public; is, therefore, interested in Local Service and is, on that account, expanding in size; and has a non-academic top administration. The *IHE* has resisted the effort by Professionalized Faculty to convert it from the Harmony-Maximizing objective to the Prestige-Maximizing objective.

The implications of this model for the operation of the U.S. system of higher education during the decade of the 1960's are clear. From the model, we would expect the system to expand its non-elite capacity (its number of student places in *IHE*s maintaining value homogeneity about non-intellectual values) by expanding its public *IHE*s both in size

UNITED STATES SYSTEM OF HIGHER EDUCATION 71

and in number. The model also predicts that the system would expand its elite capacity by converting a number of good schools into elite schools, schools dedicated to maintaining value homogeneity about intellectual values. A statistical test of the degree of association between percent expansion in size of *IHE*s over the decade and a variable representing %*PF* revealed a high association between high %*PF* and low percent Expansion, and between low %*PF* and high percent Expansion. In addition, the schools with low expansion percentages were primarily private, non-sectarian *IHE*s, whereas *IHE*s with high percentages of expansion were publicly controlled.

THE GENERAL EQUILIBRIUM SYSTEM

As indicated by Hypotheses 3 and 5, and by the models in Figures 9, 10, and 11, value homogeneity is essential to the efficient production of whatever objective an *IHE* is maximizing. The socioeconomic method of model construction leads its user to search for the prerequisite that must be met if the system being analyzed is to operate with stability and effectiveness. The essential functional prerequisite in the operation of the system of higher education is value homogeneity about those values and orientations necessary to the maximization of either of the polar objectives. Thus, as a first approximation to the equilibrium condition, we may state that the system will constantly tend to bring the Actual degree of Value Homogeneity equal to the Required degree of Value Homogeneity. This means that when Actual is less than Required, forces are set in motion to raise the Actual degree of Value Homogeneity, and when Actual is greater than Required, forces will operate to lower the Actual degree of Value Homogeneity. The operation of this equilibrium system is illustrated in Figure 12. The functional relationships composing the model are as follows:

1. $AVH = f(EHE)$. Actual Value Homogeneity is a function of Enrollment in Higher Education, *ceteris paribus*. The essential parameter within the *ceteris paribus* condition is the number of student places in the system. Given the capacity of the system, increases in enrollment permit Prestige-Maximizing *IHE*s to be more selective, thus increasing value homogeneity about intellectual values. Increased selectivity forces a number of quite intellectually-oriented students into *IHE*s attempting to maintain value homogeneity about non-intellectual values, however. The overall effect, as reflected in Curve *AA* of Part A, Figure 12, is that value homogeneity increases, but at a diminishing rate, as enrollment increases.

72 SOCIOECONOMIC METHODS

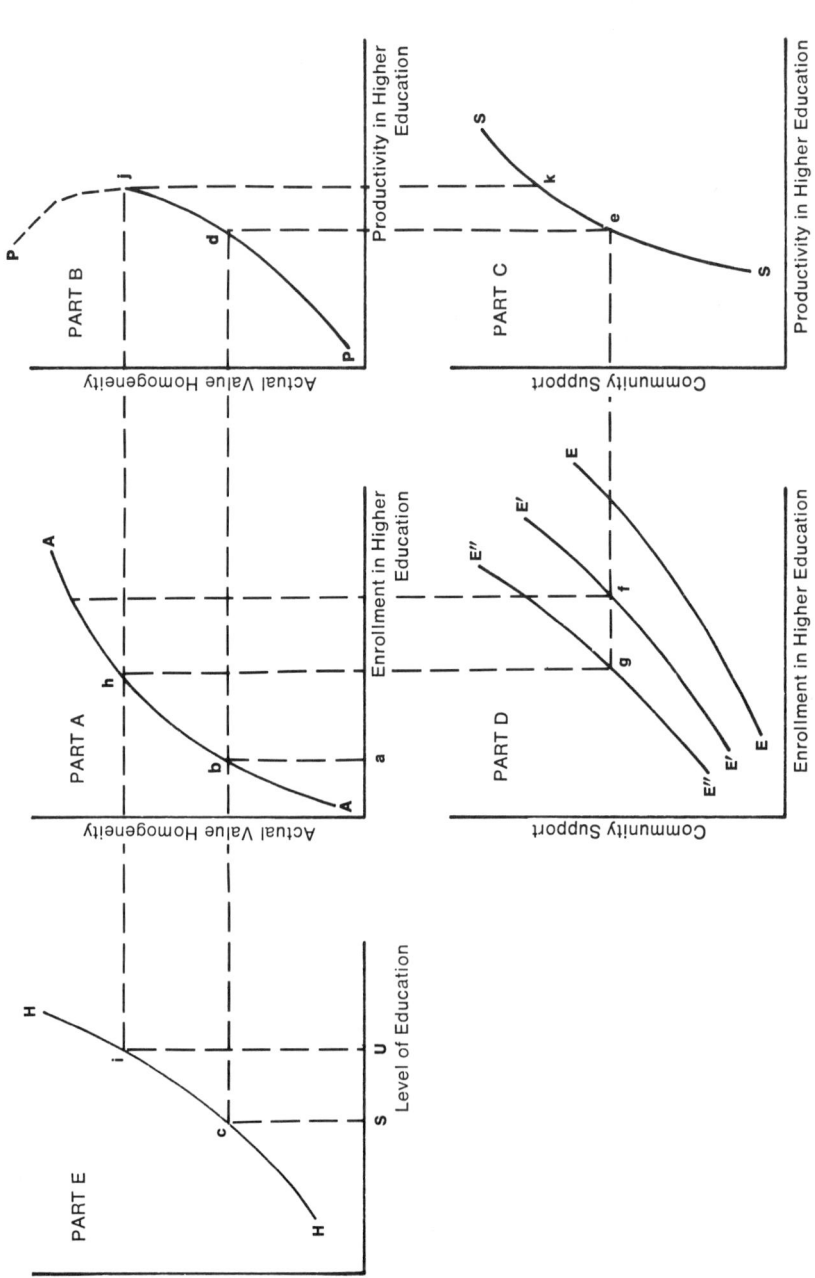

UNITED STATES SYSTEM OF HIGHER EDUCATION 73

2. $PHE = f(AVH)$. Productivity in Higher Education is a function of the Actual degree of Value Homogeneity. As *IHE*s increase in value homogeneity, they become more definitely Harmony or Prestige Maximizers, and, as such, they are more efficient as producers of their primary objective. Curve *PP* of Part B, the Productivity Function, embodies the hypothesis that as *AVH* increases there is a range in which the return to increments of *AVH* in terms of increments of induced increases in *PHE* is fairly constant. The range of constant returns is followed by a period of diminishing returns.

Although it is easy to justify the positive relationship between *AVH* and *PHE*, it is not so easy to advance a clear argument for the changes in slope shown in the *PP* Curve. The stage of diminishing returns is based upon the assumption that the faculty and physical plant of each *IHE* in the system are being held more or less constant. Given these fixed factors, increasing value homogeneity through changes in the composition of the student body may well result in diminishing returns, or even, after some point, negative returns, as indicated by the backward bending, dashed portion of the curve. One might want to argue for an initial stage of increasing returns to increases in *AVH*; this, however, would assume a level of sensitivity of the overall system to *AVH* that we do not believe exists. Assuming increasing returns in the initial stage would not affect the basic system. It would, however, tend to make the movement to equilibrium occur more quickly.

A third functional relationship deals with Community Support:

3. $CS = f(PHE)$. Community Support is a function of Productivity in Higher Education, *ceteris paribus*.

The Community comprises many constituencies, some of which, for ideological reasons, find it in their interest to support Harmony-Maximizing *IHE*s, and some of which find a display of support for *IHE*s maintaining value homogeneity about intellectual values and orientations to be satisfying. The types of support generated by increases in *PHE* are personal, political, and financial. Citizens will boost the college of their choice, organize groups to support a particular *IHE* or particular types of *IHE*s, give financial support directly to some *IHE*, make financial sacrifices to afford the best college for their children, and lobby at the state and national levels of government for support for higher education. Few citizens will do all of these things, but many doing at least one constitutes a high level of Community Support. Within the *ceteris paribus* condition, the level of national economic activity and the hierarchy of national priorities are held constant. A Sputnik Episode will shift the Support Function, Curve *SS* in Part C of Figure 12, upward, and the stresses of a Vietnam War as reflected in the ideological split of the 1970's will shift it downward. Such shifts mean that, for any given level of *PHE,* the resulting level of Community Support will be changed. The shape of the *SS* Curve embodies the assumption that there are diminishing returns to increases in *PHE* in terms of increases in *CS*. This assumption is based on the notion of diminishing salience of any goal in a hierarchy of goals as that goal or objective is more closely approached.

The fourth functional relationship deals with Enrollment in Higher Education:

4. *EHE=f(CS)*. Enrollment in Higher Education is a function of Community Support, *ceteris paribus*.

The *EE* Curves in Part D of Figure 12 indicate various possible Enrollment Functions relating given levels of *CS* with their associated levels of enrollment. One of the most important ways in which a community can support higher education is to orient their children toward the need for higher education and to back this orientation with the necessary resources. The principal factor held constant in the *ceteris paribus* condition is the number of people in the college-age population. Curve *EE* represents a higher number of college-age people than do Curves *E'E'* and *E"E"* in Part D. The slope of the *EE* Curves reflects the assumption that, as *CS* rises, enrollment increases, but by diminishing amounts because of a scarcity in the number of young people able and interested in college work.

Another functional relationship concerns Required Value Homogeneity:

5. *RVH=f(LE)*. Required Value Homogeneity is a function of the Level of Education, *ceteris paribus*.

The *HH* Function in Part E of Figure 12 illustrates the hypothesis that as children grow older they come to hold certain sets of values and orientations with increasing firmness, which requires, for their maximal educational benefit, that they be grouped according to these values and orientations. At the elementary level value homogeneity is of very low importance insofar as it conditions the ability of the teacher to effectively communicate basic skills to the students. As the child moves toward adulthood, however, value homogeneity is increasingly important as it conditions the ability of the school to communicate effectively with the students; this is reflected in the slope of the Homogeneity Function. The level of *RVH* for the efficient functioning of the secondary level of education is indicated by Point *c* on Curve *HH*. Point *i* indicates the *RVH* level needed at the College or University level. Point *c* might be considered the *RVH* level needed at the start of the eleventh grade and Point *i* the *RVH* level needed in the third year of college. Within *ceteris paribus* is the given degree to which the level of abstractness increases as the level of education increases. If, overall, there is little progression in the level of abstractness from year to year as a child moves through the system, this will be reflected in a rather flat *HH* Curve. If, on the other hand, the level of abstractness differs greatly in Harmony-Maximizing as opposed to Prestige-Maximizing *IHE*s, which may be supposed to be the case, then value homogeneity about these differing orientations to abstraction is critically important to the functioning of the system. Because of the two systems in American higher education, the *HH* Curve is rather steep. In the context of Chapter IV, learning is maximized when the conceptual level of the curriculum is matched to one that best fits the student body's orientation to abstraction, and there can be a best fit only where there is homogeneity in orientation (or ability).[7]

In the balance equation is the final relationship of the model:

6. $AVH = RVH$. Actual Value Homogeneity tends to equal Required Value Homogeneity, *ceteris paribus*.

Equation 6 states the basic tendency of the system in much the same way as $S = D$ states the basic tendency of the market model of supply and demand. The tendency specified in Equation 6 is the most fundamental tendency in the system, organizing all other tendencies. Its existence is, in fact, what makes the system a system. It is the equilibrium condition toward which the system will move when conditions exogenous to the system so permit. That $AVH = RVH$, or tends toward such an equality, is a functional prerequisite of the system of higher education as it is structured in the United States and in most other countries of the world. The expectations of all those who are a part of the system of higher education is that the requisite degree of value homogeneity will exist to some reasonable approximation. It is the knowledge of the kind of value homogeneity represented by the different kinds of *IHE*s that, under ideal conditions, guides the allocation of individuals entering and within the system of higher education to their most efficient point of utilization (or employment).

[7] To the degree that neighborhoods tend to be value-homogeneous, neighborhood schools tend to have value-homogeneous student bodies.

The operation of the model is as follows: Beginning at Point *a* in Part A of Figure 12, we note that this low level of enrollment results in a rather low level of Actual Value Homogeneity, indicated by Point *b* on Curve *AA*. We can infer excess capacity in the system from the fact that *a* level of enrollment leads to a level of *AVH* no greater than that required for the acceptable operation of the secondary level of education, which level is indicated by Point *c* on the *HH* Curve of Part E. Excess capacity leads all *IHE*s to compete for students in an effort to survive, thus causing a general lowering of admissions standards and a rather heterogeneous mixture of students within the system of higher education.

The *b* level of *AVH* (in Part B) causes the level of Productivity to reach the *d* level, which, although relatively low, is yet great enough, given the position of the *SS* Curve in Part C, to generate Community Support at the *e* level. This level of Support, interacting with the potential supply of college students, leads to an increase in Enrollment from the *a* level to the *g* level. This increase in enrollment makes it possible, given present capacity, for *IHE*s to be more selective in their admissions policies, thus generating an increase in *AVH* from the *b* level to the *h* level, indicated in Part A.

The system has now reached the *AVH* level required for acceptable (or satisfactory) operation of the system of higher education, indicated by Point *i* on the *HH* Curve of Part E. The *h* level of *AVH* raises Productivity to the *j* level, shown in Part B; this level of productivity raises the level of Community Support and, if followed through Parts D and A, will result in a level of *AVH* greater than that required for the satisfactory operation of the system.

Linking this model with the dynamic model of *IHE* conversion shown in Figure 11, we note that the system's response to Excess Homogeneity is the conversion of some *IHE*s to elite status, to Prestige Maximization, and, through high community financial support, the expansion of Harmony-Maximizing capacity. The expansion of capacity is reflected in the model as a parametric change shifting the *AA* Curve in Part A to the right. To illustrate this dynamic tendency of the system to expand its capacity once $AVH=RVH$, we might think of the *AA* Curve as becoming horizontal once it reaches the *RVH* level; the horizontal portion comprises the points generated by successive rightward shifts of the *AA* Function. Thus, through the process of rightward shifts of the *AA* Function, there is a tendency for the system to maintain the *AVH* at about the Required level of Value Homogeneity.

The situation we have just examined approximates what obtained during the decade of the 1960's. In the early 1970's, however, the system was faced with the necessity of adjusting to a downward shift in the *SS*

Curve, partly because of economic stress and partly because of ideological shifts, and to a change in demographic trends, resulting in a leftward shift of the *EE* Curve. The impact of both these exogeneous shifts resulted in a sizable reduction in enrollment and in the levels of *AVH* and Productivity. The proper system response is a leftward shift in the *AA* Curve; that is, the correct remedy is the closing of excess capacity. The system resists closing its units, however, and we return to the conditions associated with Point *a,* those being a state of excess capacity accompanied by lowered admissions standards and, perhaps, the closing of a number of financially weak *IHE*s.

As is true of most social systems, including the economy, the spontaneous mechanisms of adjustment charged with the maintenance of equilibrium conditions seem to function better during periods of expansion than they do during periods of contraction.

SOCIAL WELFARE EVALUATIONS

Making normative judgments about the social welfare implications of the operation of any social system has, in the case of economics, come to be enclosed or circumscribed by certain ground rules. Chief among these rules is that the evaluator takes the present social system as a given. For example, welfare economics attempts to demonstrate that the market system maximizes social welfare because it tends, under certain conditions, to maximize the market value of the Gross National Product, and more market value is always to be preferred to less. The economist takes as his givens the distribution of income, the tastes and preferences of consumers, and, of course, an economy of coordinated, efficiently operating markets.

A sociologist may think that an efficient economy is one that tends to equalize the distribution of income by systematically operating to eliminate the force of ascriptive factors in the shaping of an individual's opportunity set and might, in the stationary state case, take the GNP as given. A social psychologist or a political scientist would, doubtless, have a somewhat different slant on the normative aspects of the operation of any given social subsystem. The point is that some set of factors must be taken as given, as setting the framework within which the system is to be evaluated.

In the case of the system of higher education, what should be the givens taken as setting the basic framework? A fair approach to this question might be to ask just what it is that we really expect of our system of higher education. If the system produces, in an efficient way (and to know the efficient way requires that one first know a great deal about the education production function), the things we really expect of it, then it must, following the logic of the welfare approach, be seen as maximizing social welfare.

There is much literature, some of it objective and some of it normatively critical, that shows that students are little affected in their values and orientations by their higher education. There appears to be some impact in the area of values and orientations, but it is not large nor, according to some studies, is it long lasting, resistant to the pressures of the adult world. Some *IHE*s say that they have as their objective the communication of lasting values, but most do not. The real question is, from the analytical point of view, do we really expect or want a system of higher education that spends a great part of its resources on value and orientation modification? The system developed in this chapter is one that operates to produce and communicate knowledge, and it would appear that this is exactly what this society really expects of its institutions of higher education. In satisfying the socially desired objectives, a system organized around the dual goals of Harmony and Prestige Maximization appears to produce *IHE* behavior that is quite efficient in its achievement of the socially desired objectives. This efficiency is primarily achieved by grouping people according to their values and orientations, such that each *IHE* represents a homogeneous set of values and orientations. Such groupings are, according to our analysis, the most efficient way to produce and communicate knowledge. Thus, we may conclude that the system ranks high in terms of its advancement of the social welfare, given our criteria.

Part Three
ORGANIZATION THEORETIC CONSIDERATIONS

Chapter VI

A MODEL OF ORGANIZATIONAL DEVELOPMENT APPLIED TO A SCHOOL*

Organization development (OD) is the systematic application of social psychological knowledge to the planning and implementation of change in the set of spontaneous mutual interactions that constitute the human dynamics of a formal organization, to the end that the organization perform its tasks more effectively and more creatively, and, some would add, more humanely.

One OD team has expressed the interests of OD specialists in the following way:

> Many problems arise in the shifting psychological contact between man and organization. Are the parties thinking in terms of simply a job or of a career? How much emotional commitment to organi-

---

* For aid in the development of the analysis in this chapter, I would like to express my indebtedness to the members of the 1971 Seminar on the Social Psychology of Change at Teachers College, Columbia University, and particularly to my research associates, Linda Peller and Barbara Haynes.

zational goals is offered and expected? What balance is struck between dependence and independence, between conformity and creativity, between duty and self-expression? Is the organization accumulating a reservoir of trained human assets and good will, or is it dissipating human resources built up in an earlier period? What is being done to anticipate and provide for the talents necessary to implement new strategies attuned to environmental change? [1]

In preparing to answer these questions through systematic analysis, the authors of the quotation attempt to divide their concerns into three broad areas of contact or interface: between the Organization and its Environment, between Groups within the Organization, and, finally, between the Individual and the Organization.

Although most OD specialists agree that the three interface approach is useful, we will attempt to show that this division, even for expositional purposes, is dysfunctional when the purpose is to generate new knowledge directed to organizational development. If OD is to mature into a science, then, it may be maintained, it must come to have a method for determining the critical interrelationships among components of the organization, such that predictions can be made about the impact of any parametric change the OD specialist engineers with the full knowledge and understanding of the client system.

THE SOCIOECONOMIC METHOD IN ORGANIZATIONAL DEVELOPMENT

There are almost as many OD techniques as there are change agents in the business of selling change to problem-ridden client organizations. This observation, along with the observation that the interventions of a given OD specialist tend to vary widely in the degree of success achieved, has prompted some social psychologists, most notably Professor Harvey Hornstein of Columbia University, to undertake the task of systematically analyzing the techniques of given change agents to determine the social psychological principles upon which each implicitly bases his OD approach and, thereby, to generate the set of necessary preconditions within the client organization leading to a high probability of success for a given change agent. The fundamental hypothesis underlying Hornstein's approach is that, under conditions that can be specified, a specific technique operating upon discoverable social psychological principles,

---

[1] Paul R. Lawrence and Jay W. Lorsch, *Developing Organizations: Diagnosis and Action* (Reading, Mass.: Addison-Wesley, 1969), p. 7.

will, in the hands of a particular change agent, yield desirable (or the desired) effects.

One of the striking aspects of social psychology, at least to one trained in economics, is the degree to which social psychologists atomize their research findings. That is, because social psychology is experimentally oriented, the research produced deals with the results of tests of very narrow and quite well defined hypotheses. These hypotheses, many of which are like those advanced in the previous chapter, are, potentially, the building blocks needed in the construction of models of social systems, but the discipline has yet to move strongly in the direction of utilizing its rich store of tested hypotheses in the construction of complex systems. The principal purpose of this chapter is to illustrate how the wealth of social psychology might be used to construct complex systems through application of the socioeconomic method. We will concentrate on the OD work of one individual, Mr. X, as he dealt with secondary schools.

THE MODEL

Mr. X was interviewed according to a standardized form developed by Professor Hornstein. We then read a number of reports on school interventions written by Mr. X, and a number of articles written by others on Mr. X's technique. This led to development of a socioeconomic model that represented the causal framework implicit in Mr. X's approach to OD. That is, the model is a representation of the causal connections leading to organizational development that appear to inform Mr. X's actions. Mr. X, in other words, behaved *as if* he understood this model and sought to bring about change by using the model as his basic guide to action.

The model is shown in Figure 13; following are the functional relationships composing the system:

1. $SE = f(CB)$. Self-esteem is a function of Collaborative Behavior, *ceteris paribus*.

We could make reference to the literature on Own versus Induced Motivation within the context of Cooperative versus Competitive social environments to explain the functional relationship shown in Part A of Figure 13. The explanation advanced here for the impact of Collaborative Behavior on Self-esteem, however, is based on the work of Kahn, Wolfe, et al.[2] Role ambiguity stems from inadequate information about

[2] R. L. Kahn, D. M. Wolfe, R. P. Quinn, and J. D. Snoek, *Organizational Stress: Studies in Role Conflict and Ambiguity* (New York: John Wiley & Sons, 1964).

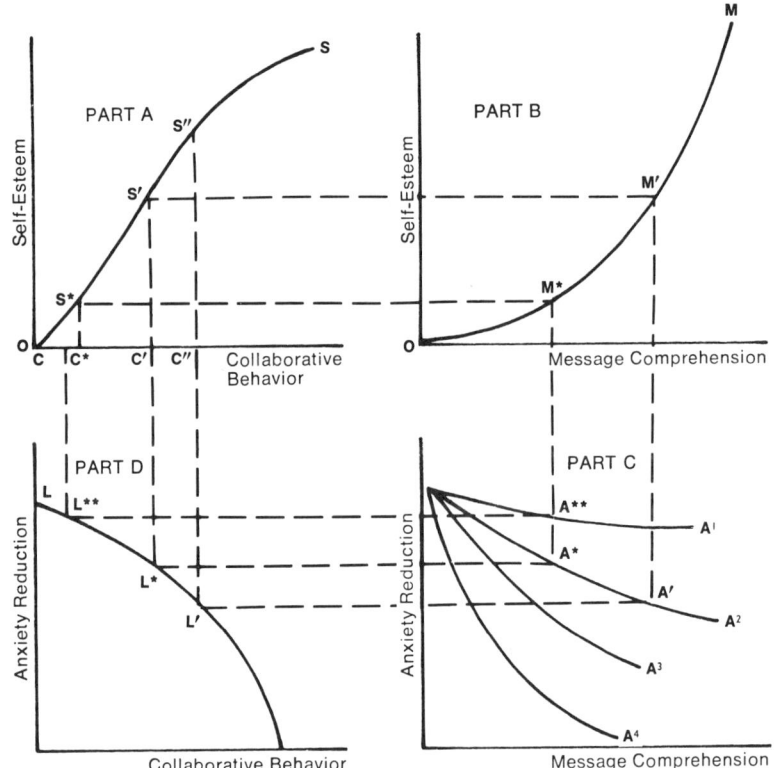

FIGURE 13. A Model of the Social Psychological Dynamics of a School

what is to be done in a given role, how it is to be done, and how it is to be evaluated. Thus, "role ambiguity is a direct function of the discrepancy between the information available to the person and that which is required for adequate performance of his role."[3] Further,

> Ambiguity leads to increased emotional tension and decreased satisfaction with one's job. It also contributes significantly to a sense of futility and to a loss of self-confidence [and self-esteem]. Conclusions about the personal costs of ambiguity are well supported statistically.[4]

Mr. X's implicit hypothesis is that the school in trouble is a school in which individuals have suffered severe losses in self-esteem because of

---
[3] *Ibid.*, p. 73.
[4] *Ibid.*, p .85.

role ambiguity, particularly the ambiguity resulting from inadequate evaluative information. This inadequacy is raised to crisis levels by high rates of community change. Bringing about an increase in the level of collaborative activity generates new statuses and new roles for existing statuses as well as a high level of spontaneously sent evaluative information. In competitively structured situations, there is a degree of isolation that prohibits ongoing role sending activity, activity that, through interpersonal interaction, contains substantial amounts of evaluative feedback.

The shape of the Self-esteem Function, Curve OS in Part A of Figure 13, reflects the hypothesis that increases in Collaborative Behavior (CB) will at first produce increasing returns to Self-esteem due to the individual's need for and sensitivity to constructive evaluative feedback. As the level of Collaborative Behavior rises and the intensity of the need for evaluative information diminishes, so too does the impact of CB on Self-esteem, resulting in an extended range of positive but diminishing returns. Thus, the Self-esteem production function has a stage of increasing returns, followed by a stage of diminishing returns.

The rate of change in the school's environmental context is the most important parameter underlying the position of the Self-esteem Function and held constant within the *ceteris paribus* condition. Rapid change in the community served by a school will lower Curve OS because of the impact social change has on established role expectations. Most of the schools with which Mr. X works are schools in crisis due to urban change.

2. $MC = f(SE)$. Message Comprehension is a function of the level of Self-esteem.

In Part B of Figure 13 we postulate, through the shape of Curve OM, a relationship between Self-esteem and Message Comprehension such that increases in SE lead to diminishing increases in MC. The messages involved in Message Comprehension are those sent between collaborating individuals. As we have noted, collaboration is particularly effective within organizations because it permits specialization without isolation. That is, collaboration reduces role ambiguity by spontaneously producing and distributing information about goals (what is to be done), methods for attaining goals (how it is to be done), and evaluative feedback (how the group is doing, rather than how the competitively positioned individual is doing).

Research on message comprehension indicates that only those with relatively high self-esteem can understand (receive) the messages spontaneously generated as part of the interpersonal interaction that true collaboration demands. There is a great deal of research on the effects of such personality variables as anxiety and self-esteem on the process of persuasion and attitude change, much of which is summarized in an article by Stanley Lehmann.[5] Lehmann sees opinion and behavior change as occurring in a "multi-step process involving at least (a) reception of the message and (b) yielding to it."[6] Lehmann demonstrates that anxiety relates "negatively to reception of the message and positively to yielding to it, while self-esteem is likely to be negatively related to yielding and positively to reception."[7] Thus, given a high state of organizationally experienced anxiety, increased self-esteem aids in the process of inducing dynamic, self-sustaining, organizational change by facilitating receipt of messages.

The hypothesis implicit in Mr. X's effort to increase self-esteem as the first step in developing the school (how he accomplishes this will be treated at a later point in this chapter) is that development cannot begin until individuals begin to communicate, and individuals cannot communicate and will not communicate if, in a crisis situation, they do not first experience a rise in their self-esteem. Further, when the rise in self-esteem is collectively experienced, a phenomenon Mr. X attempts to engineer, it facilitates the growth of collaborative norms, of trust.

3. $AR = f(MC)$. Anxiety Reduction is a function of increasing Message Comprehension, *ceteris paribus*.

When an individual is part of a group within which there is a high level of message comprehension, the group will have a sense of its purpose and the individual will understand his part in the attainment of that purpose. Anxiety results from an individual's inability to structure his situation cognitively; that is, anxiety results from role ambiguity. The statistical investigations of Kahn, Wolfe, *et al.*, have shown a "substantial association between experienced ambiguity and tension scores."[8] The authors go on to point out that this association is very much influenced, in the individual case, by one's need for cognition, defined as

> ... a need to structure relevant situations in meaningful, integrated ways. It is a need to understand and make reasonable the experiential world. "Meaningfulness" and integration are individually defined in that they vary with the person's past experience

---

[5] Stanley Lehmann, "Personality and Compliance: A Study of Anxiety and Self-esteem in Opinion and Behavior Change," *Journal of Personality and Social Psychology*, 15 (March 1970), pp. 76-86.
[6] *Ibid.*, pp. 76-77.
[7] *Ibid.*, p. 77.
[8] Kahn, Wolfe, Quinn, and Snoek, *Organizational Stress*, p. 87.

and capacity for such integration. For any given individual different situations will be differentially important for the arousal and satisfaction of the need.[9]

The Anxiety-Reduction Functions of Part C illustrate the hypothesized relationship between increases in *MC* and reductions in Anxiety. The mechanism of reduction is increased cognitive structuring made possible through increased Message Comprehension. Within the *ceteris paribus* condition is the average need for cognition of the individuals composing the school. The different Anxiety-Reduction Functions shown all share the basic characteristic that increases in *MC* lead to diminishing reductions in anxiety. The hypothesis embodied in the shape of the curves is that the psychological impact of the first movements toward cognitive structuring can be expected to be greater than successive improvements in cognitive structuring produce, this because the first movements can usually be expected to deal with setting up a basic mental framework, whereas those occurring later will be primarily limited to refinements. The reason for showing a number of curves is that a given level of message comprehension may be expected, over time, to lead to progressive cognitive structuring. Thus, in the short run, cognitive structuring and the resulting reduction in anxiety will be shown by movement along a given curve, but in the longer run, the curve itself will shift downward because of the progressive working up of the cognitive structure on the basis of any given level of Message Comprehension. For example, given an *MC* level of M^*, shown in Part B, the level of reduction in anxiety will, at first, be A^{**}, shown on Curve A^1 of Part C. Even if *MC* remains unchanged, however, anxiety will fall to the A^* level due to the progressive structuring that can occur at the given level of Message Comprehension.

4. $CB = f(AR)$. Collaborative Behavior is a function of Anxiety Reduction, *ceteris paribus*.

Curve *LL* in Part D of Figure 13 is the Leadership Function; it shows how the energy released when anxiety is reduced can, under certain circumstances, be directed into increases in Collaborative Behavior when Leaders are prepared to so direct it. Mr. X's strategy in aiding a school to achieve self-sustaining development importantly involves training and prior positioning of leaders within the school. Implicitly, he seems to

---

[9] *Ibid.*, p. 87, quoting A. Cohen, E. Stotland, and D. Wolfe, "An Experimental Investigation of Need for Cognition," *Journal of Abnormal and Social Psychology,* 51 (January 1955), p. 291.

understand that psychic energy is made available for channeling toward organizational objectives at the moment it is released from anxiety maintenance. The formulation of this hypothesis, implicit in Mr. X's behavior, is based on the work of A. M. Shimkunas:

> . . . it can be reasonably stated that individuals high in anxiety appear to be predisposed toward acting upon the immediacies of the situation, overreacting to both success and failure.
>
> While reactivity to recent experience may be a function of their greater sensitivity to important situational cues, it also tends to magnify the import of subsequent experiences that differ from the most immediate one. The tendency may facilitate [functionally adaptive] behavior by increasing the individual's motivation and awareness of the environment.[10]

From Shimkunas, we conclude that, as the level of anxiety falls, it becomes increasingly difficult to lead individuals into new undertakings. This conclusion is reflected in the shape of the Leadership Function, which shows ever smaller increases in Collaborative Behavior in response to successive increments in Anxiety Reduction. In addition, as anxiety is progressively reduced, there is less and less freed energy made available to leadership for channeling into Collaborative Behavior. Furthermore, the rising levels of Self-esteem that were the cause of increased Message Comprehension (which, in turn, reduced anxiety) tend to make individuals more discerning in what they will and will not do.

From the standpoint of the Change Agent operating on the basis of this model, the most critical aspect of the intervention following his entrance technique is preparation of the leadership needed to complete the self-sustaining cycle. The organization must be prepared to increase the number of its leadership positions as a part of its overall commitment to an increase in collaborative behavior, a commitment that must be obtained at the point of entrance. Before we discuss the entry technique, however, two more aspects of the model remain to be explained: the dynamics of the interaction of the four functional relationships making up the model, and the emergent properties of the social system created by this dynamic process.

Let us assume that the entry technique has been successful; success is defined as inducing an increase in Collaborative Behavior from zero to the C^* level, as indicated in Part A. The C^* level will induce an increase

---

[10] A. M. Shimkunas, "Anxiety and Expectancy Change: The Effects of Failure and Uncertainty," *Journal of Personality and Society Psychology, 15* (March 1970), p. 40.

in the level of Self-esteem to the S^*level, which, as shown in Part B, will raise Message Comprehension from the zero or near zero level to the M^* level. If the school is frozen by its anxiety, the intervention will fail. Curve A^1 of Part C is the Anxiety-Reduction Function of a school frozen by its anxiety. Note that the amount of AR produced by the M^* level of MC is inadequate to permit the leadership to work an increase in CB. This result is shown in Part D, where the A^{**} level of AR intersects the Leadership Function at Point L^{**}, leading to a sustainable level of Collaborative Behavior below that engineered by the Change Agent at the time of its initial intervention, indicated by Point c in Part A. Thus we come upon one of the necessary preconditions for Mr. X's technique to be successful, that is, that the level of anxiety must not be too great or the collaborative-behavior approach to OD will not produce the expected results. If the operative Anxiety-Reduction Function is A^2, or any of the other AR Functions indicated in Part C, the intervention will succeed, provided the leaders are trained and positioned. If we assume that Curve A^2 is the effective AR Function, then the A^* level of AR will be induced by the M^* level of MC. Given the position of the Leadership Function, this will lead to a sustainable level of Collaborative Behavior greater than that originally induced at the point of intervention; this level is shown in Part A as the C' level of CB. The path generated by successive iterations of this process is indicated in Figure 13.

We now come to the question of what, sociologically speaking, is happening in a school or other formal organization that is developing along the lines indicated by this model. What is happening to the hierarchical structure and to the norms in operation as progressive increases in Collaborative Behavior take place, and in what way does this constitute development?

Hierarchically speaking, the additional leadership positions Mr. X's intervention seeks to create are both vertical links between the established positions within the hierarchy and horizontal extensions of the established levels within the hierarchy. Implicit in his approach to OD is the hypothesis that individuals are more productive, more creative, when they have expanded opportunities for social exchange within the organization; for it is through social exchange that most individuals find meaningful existential satisfactions.

Because Collaborative Behavior increases the opportunities for social exchange, and because social exchange can be such an important aspect of organizational development, the notion must be given some detailed attention prior to our discussion of the means used by Mr. X in engineering its systematic increase. We may begin by separating the sociological from the psychological aspects of social exchange:

To be sure, each individual's behavior is reinforced by the rewards it brings, but the psychological process of reinforcement does not suffice to explain the exchange relationship that develops. This social relation is the joint product of the actions of both individuals, with the actions of each being dependent on those of the other. The emergent properties of social exchange consequent to this interdependence cannot be accounted for by the psychological processes that motivate the behavior of the parties.[11]

Skilled leaders can, by operating on the basis of collaboration, so influence the social structure and norms of the school that the principal emergent property of the increase in social exchange is the norm of collaboration. When the norm of collaboration is in force, individuals are rewarded by social approval for actions in support of the group; social approval, rather than material reward, becomes the prized coin.

A school in which each teacher and administrator produces certain socially (or organizationally) isolated behaviors in exchange for money is not unlike many other types of organizations in Western society and, if the parallel may be pardoned, is not unlike a mental hospital in which behavior is modified through the installation of a contingency structure involving the use of a token economy. Such programs are incapable of producing a developing social system, one capable of generating emergent properties functional to the goals of the organization. The following quotation, on the other hand, reports the results of an experiment conducted by G. W. Fairweather, *et al.*, in which community development was achieved through the use of social exchange rather than monetary (or token) rewards:

> In the task-group condition an incentive system was applied in which the participants received increasing monetary and pass privilege rewards, contingent on the development of four levels of progressively complex social and self-directive behavior. The responsibility for evaluating and modifying the behavior of each member, and for implementing the incentive system, was delegated to the group. . . .
> The voluminous data from this ambitious, well-executed field study demonstrate that the program specifically designed to reinstate interpersonal responsiveness [read "social exchange"] and self-directive behavior in patients yielded consistently superior outcomes. Patients in [the group-condition as contrasted with the traditional token system] rapidly formed cohesive groups, in which

---

[11] Peter M. Blau, *Exchange and Power in Social Life* (New York: John Wiley & Sons, 1967), p. 4.

the members exhibited increasing mutual interest, help, and responsibility. They organized their own employment group, interviewed and counseled patients, and assumed full responsibility in locating employment for eligible members. They also established informal educational programs taught by group members who possessed specialized skills or knowledge. . . . The investigators report that the monetary and pass privilege rewards were essential in the early phase of treatment, but after the patients established mutually rewarding relationships with each other, pride in their accomplishments, competitiveness with other groups, and mutual social approval and disapproval became the major reinforcing events regulating their day-to-day behavior.[12]

The parallels between Fairweather's project and Mr. X's school intervention are striking. In the case of a school, the crisis is the prerequisite early phase motivator, equivalent in function to Fairweather's use of monetary and pass privilege rewards as the means of beginning the group toward self-sustaining development. As with the hospital, the crude motivator ceases to be necessary once mutually rewarding social exchanges develop.

In Fairweather's program, as in Mr. X's, the progressive development of complex social and self-directive behavior depends upon the emergence of leaders from among the members of the group; that is, the group selects its own leadership, thus giving the leadership an original grant of legitimacy, legitimacy that can be maintained only so long as the rewards of the voluntary association exceed the costs of compliance with the leader's demands. Examples of the types of leadership positions Mr. X seeks to see created are a committee on student-faculty relations, a committee on school-police relations, a committee on faculty-administration relations, and a committee on student discipline. The object of all these committees is to knit the members of the school and of the community together by locating points of conflict and contact and making these points sources of personal satisfaction through social exchange.

THE ENTRY TECHNIQUE

The purpose of the Entry is to set up the Leadership Function shown in Part D of Figure 13, to increase Self-esteem to the critical minimum,

---

[12] Albert Bandura, *Principles of Behavior Modification* (New York: Holt, Rinehart and Winston, 1969), pp. 269-271, citing G. W. Fairweather, D. H. Sanders, H. Maynard, and D. L. Cressler, *Community Life for the Mentally Ill: An Alternative to Institutional Care* (Chicago: Aldine, 1969).

and to ignite the change process. To accomplish these goals, Mr. X must create an ignition system, one that fires off the developmental process and then vanishes. The Entry (or Ignition) System engineered by Mr. X has four basic components: Valid Information, Self-esteem, Opinion Change, and Action. Given the psychological driving force of the crisis facing the school, these four system components work together in a chain-like reaction; that is, Valid Information generates a rapid rise in the Self-esteem of the leaders of the school, the administrators, leading teachers, and staff. The rise in Self-esteem facilitates Opinion Change, and the combination of Valid Information, increased Self-esteem, and changed opinion leads to Action directed toward the creation of the Leadership Function. Following ignition, the Entry System vanishes and the more stable set of functional relationships shown in Figure 13 takes over. A prevading sense of crisis is the motive force underlying the chain reaction Entry System, whereas a receding sense of crisis and a reduction in the level of Anxiety power the developmental system. Given Mr. X's approach to OD, therefore, his interventions will have the highest probability of success in situations in which there is a crisis. As has been pointed out, however, the sense of crisis, the level of Anxiety, must not be too high, or the school will be frozen in its anxiety.

SOME METHODOLOGICAL CONSIDERATIONS

On the surface, the model of school development illustrated by Figure 13 and the model of *IHE* Conversion shown in Figure 11 may appear to be of the same basic type. Inasmuch as this is not the case, a comparison of the two may lead to a better understanding of each.

The two systems represented by the two models differ most obviously and most essentially in the matter of their origin. The *IHE* model represents a system that, under given parametric conditions, will develop in any *IHE* and is, therefore, a part of a larger equilibrium-seeking system. That is, the *IHE* model is a component in a microsocietal system and cannot be viewed apart from that system. The school OD model represents a system that, under given parametric conditions, can be created through the intervention of a Change Agent. The model is not a component in a larger system, but rather is a representation of a possible set of interrelationships that may come into being within a particular organization. In addition, although the organization that has been used as our example is a school, there is nothing in the model limiting it to schools.

Although the *IHE* model is not an equilibrium model, it is part of an equilibrium-seeking system. The school OD model is not an equilibrium model, it is a process model or system. In an equilibrium-seeking system there must be a specified equilibrium condition, such as is represented by the balance equations in most of our previous models. In our discussion of dynamic equilibrium models in Chapter II, we noted that what makes a model dynamic is the specification of the path the system traces as it tends toward the equilibrium condition. Thus, when the system is displaced from the equilibrium condition by some posited change in parametric conditions, the path back to the stable condition can be shown, which, in some cases, may be a stable rate of change or growth. In the school OD model, however, there is no specified balance to be struck between opposing forces, there is nothing functionally prerequisite. The process of development simply continues until any one of a number of contingencies occurs to interrupt the process.

Finally, the two models differ in the basic motive force underlying the causal sequence. In macrosocietal and microsocietal models, the key variables are the products of the operation of complex social structures. In organization theoretic models, the key variables are derived from the operation of social psychological structures derived from the presence or absence of a social exchange process. For example, in the model of *IHE* conversion, the basic component variable was Percent Professionalized Faculty. The process whereby faculty become professionalized is that of socialization as accomplished by the elite graduate schools. Elite undergraduate schools may begin the process, or take it up where the intellectually oriented family and/or community leaves off, but, in the last analysis, the responsibility for deep socialization into the scholarly values and orientations rests with the elite graduate departments. In the case of the model of school OD, the basic variable was Collaborative Behavior, which, if truly collaborative, will raise any individual's Self-esteem, almost without regard to his prior socialization. Thus, the motive force directing the behavior of individuals in the school OD model was the reinforcement or reward of rising Self-esteem, a product of collaborative social exchange, whereas the motive force in the *IHE* conversion model was increased Prestige, a reward produced by the operation of a complex social structure. In each case, the individual actors knew exactly what sorts of actions were necessary if the reward was to be gained, but how very different the source of the reinforcement!

Chapter VII

A SOCIOECONOMIC MODEL OF CLASSROOM COMMUNICATION

With this model, we not only complete the examples of applied socioeconomic method presented in this study, but we also carry the technique to the least complex level yet considered, the classroom. At this sub-organizational level, the method that has been applied in the preceding chapters takes on a substantially different character. Although it shares the organizational theoretic characteristic of dependence upon social exchange for its motive force, it fails to achieve the degree of integration of methods drawn from economics and sociology (or, in some cases, economics and social psychology) characteristic of the models heretofore presented.

The methods used in this model are drawn primarily from sociology and economics. The diagrammatic presentations are very much like those familiar to anyone who has studied microeconomics. The theoretical development is very much like that familiar to anyone who has studied sociology. The two disciplines are linked in this analysis through the use of constructs that are psychological in origin, but also have deep roots in the old sociology of such theorists as Charles Horton Cooley.

SOCIOLOGICAL APPROACHES TO THE PROBLEM

Existing sociological literature dealing with the classroom falls into two categories: (1) research that demonstrates the impact of extra-classroom activities and conditions on student academic performance in the classroom, such as the work of James Coleman [1] and Dael Wolfle; [2] and (2) research that takes a structural-functional approach, such as the work of Talcott Parsons [3] and Natalie Rogoff. [4] Looking at these two approaches from an input-output perspective, the first approach studies the effects of society on school inputs, mainly teacher and student values, attitudes, and need-orientations, whereas the second is directed, through a functional prerequisite orientation, to the discovery of the latent functions of formal education in the larger society.

As Parsons notes, the school class is a social system, one designed to communicate subject matter to students. Yet, strangely, the sociological aspects of the communication process have not been the subject of much research, a situation that may appear considerably less strange when one gives thought to the possibility that this may be due to the absence of a suitable method by which to bring sociological theory into the communication context.

The broad outlines of a sociology of communication may best be appreciated by contrasting the notions of communication and learning. If learning theory is seen as the theory of processes internal to the individual, with cognitive processes, then the sociology of communication may be viewed as concerning itself with (1) the approaches used by the communicator, the sender's Sociological Style of Communication (*SSC*), and (2) the impact of a particular *SSC* on the social context within which the stimuli are received by the learner.

THE SOCIOLOGICAL STYLE OF COMMUNICATION

The way in which an individual perceives or understands the individuals with whom he is attempting to communicate will influence the kinds of social exchanges that can take place between them and will, on that account, determine the sociological properties that emerge from the process of social exchange. In the problem at hand, the communicator

---

[1] James Coleman, "Academic Achievement and the Structure of Competition," *Harvard Educational Review, 29* (Fall 1959), pp. 339-351.
[2] Dael Wolfle, "Educational Opportunity, Measured Intelligence, and Social Background," in Halsey, Floud, and Anderson, eds., *Education, Economy, and Society,* pp. 216-240.
[3] Talcott Parsons, "The School Class as a Social System: Some of its Functions in American Society," *Socialization and Schools, Harvard Educational Review,* Reprint Series No. 1 (1968), pp. 69-90.
[4] Natalie Rogoff, "Local Social Structure and Educational Selection," in Halsey, Floud, and Anderson, *Education, Economy, and Society,* pp. 241-251.

is a teacher operating within the context of a classroom; insofar as we are dealing with a group having a leader in which the task involves the planned and structured communication of ideas and facts by the leader to the group, however, the situation is one found in many settings.

As a first approximation to categorizing the modes of teacher perception of students, we may use the concept of role-taking or role reversal, the ability to place oneself in the position of another. Role-taking is the most essential part of the act of communication, of explaining something to another person.

The mode of role-taking utilized by a teacher is specified by a point somewhere along a continuum between Inferential Role-Taking and Intuitional Role-Taking.[5] Inferential Role-Taking occurs when a teacher approaches his students as objects, seeking to understand them in an impersonal and objective way. The model used is behaviorism, or scientific psychology. It is human relationship in the sense of *Gesellschaft;* that is, it is Cooley's spatial knowledge, explanatory-predictive, inferential-rationalistic, impersonal-objective. Intuitional Role-Taking occurs when a teacher approaches his students as fellow human beings. His is the role-taking of the psychologist-existentialist. His understanding is the product of *verstehen;* that is, it is Cooley's social knowledge and Toennies' *Gemeinschaft.* The combination of these two types of role-taking used by a teacher and his skill in using them constitute an individual teacher's Sociological Style of Communication. As will become clear, the valued exchange commodities in the interpersonal interchange between teacher and class will differ as a function of the teacher's *SSC;* that is, as a function of the teacher's position along the role-taking continuum and his skill in the use of his sociogenetically determined combination of the two types of role-taking, *ceteris paribus.*

SOCIAL EXCHANGE IN THE CLASSROOM

Peter Blau[6] has developed an approach to sociological inquiry known as exchange theory that builds on the work of George C. Homans, and John W. Thibaut and Harold H. Kelley. To the degree that power relationships are an important part of the planned and structured communication of ideas and facts by a leader to a group (or by a teacher to a class), the exchange theory approach becomes an important component of any sociology of communication.

---

[5] In the development of our thinking on the subject of role-taking, the work of Stanley Stark, "*Gemeinschaft,* Inner Creation, and Role-Taking (Empathy): III," *Psychological Reports,* 26 (March 1970), pp. 183-210, was critical. The exposition of the types of role-taking in this paragraph has been taken directly from Stark's article.

[6] Blau, *Exchange and Power in Social Life.*

Blau sees the concept of social exchange as one that "directs attention to the emergent properties in interpersonal relations and social interaction."[7] Further, it is a type of exchange that is "limited to actions that are contingent on rewarding reactions from others and that ceases when these expected reactions are not forthcoming."[8]

Before proceeding to a consideration of how relationships develop out of social exchange, it may be helpful to give an example of the way social exchange operates in a classroom situation. Ray C. Rist, in an article titled "Student Social Class and Teacher Expectations: The Self-Fulfilling Prophecy in Ghetto Education,"[9] notes what occurs in a kindergarten class when a teacher expects that certain students will not be capable of learning or of producing any other kind of teacher-rewarding exchange commodity in return for the teacher's communication efforts:

> The organization of the kindergarten classroom according to the expectation of success or failure after the eighth day of school became the basis for the differential treatment of the children for the remainder of the school year.[10]

> The realization of the self-fulfilling prophecy within the classroom was in its final stages by late May of the kindergarten year. Lack of communication with the teacher, lack of involvement in class activities and infrequent instruction all characterized the situation of the children at Tables 2 and 3 [where the children not expected to be capable of producing rewarding reactions were seated]. The teacher devoted her attention to teaching [communicating with] those children at Table 1.[11]

It would, perhaps, be stretching the point to say that the teacher in question had an *SSC;* that is, it may be doubted that she was capable of either type or combination of the types of role-taking. The children who received her attention were, in every case, those who were well dressed. Although Rist does not make the point, it is probable that the rewards sought by this teacher in return for her efforts would generally be produced by the parents of the children, parents belonging to a high socioeconomic status, parents likely to be active in the life of the school.

---

[7] *Ibid.*, p. 4.
[8] *Ibid.*, p. 6.
[9] Ray C. Rist, "Student Social Class and Teacher Expectations: The Self-Fulfilling Prophecy in Ghetto Education," *Harvard Educational Review, 40* (August 1970), pp. 411-451.
[10] *Ibid.*, p. 423.
[11] *Ibid.*, p. 425.

Thus, the Rist quotations illustrate a situation in which the teacher is engaged in what might be termed an indirect social exchange. In such cases, there is no self-contained exchange system developing within the teacher-student relationship. In situations such as the one described by Rist, there may indeed be communication, but there is no communication system; for such a system involves a consideration of the mutual adjustments between individuals on the basis of the reactions each makes to the other.

Power in the Classroom

An important aspect of social exchange is the way in which it gives rise to power relationships. Power develops when the following conditions exist:

1. A has something B wants, but B has nothing material, in terms of normally exchangeable goods and services, to offer that is valuable to A.
2. B has no alternative source of supply. If B is to have what he needs, he must have it from A.
3. B has no way of forcing A to yield.
4. B cannot do without the thing A supplies.

If B is unable or unwilling to do without A's goods or services, cannot force A to supply the needed thing, is without alternative sources of supply, and has nothing to offer in exchange of a material or service nature of interest to A, "he must subordinate himself to the other and comply with his wishes [if he is able], thereby rewarding the other with power over himself as an inducement for furnishing the needed help." [12]

The social structure of the classroom is such that a power relationship between teacher and student is built in; that is, the student, either by enrolling in the class or by being placed in it, must, to some degree, subordinate himself to the teacher. Unlike the kindergarten example, it will be assumed that the students of our model are all able, to a greater or lesser degree, to achieve subordination, that they are able to produce teacher-rewarding reactions.

The power a teacher exercises over students is often viewed by the students as being legitimate. How that power is made legitimate, however, will differ from teacher to teacher as a function of the teacher's Sociological Style of Communication. Therefore, the *SSC* factor determines the type of teacher-rewarding reactions produced by the students

---

[12] Blau, *Exchange and Power in Social Life*, p. 22.

and the way in which the teacher achieves power viewed as legitimate by his students.

Power may also be viewed as illegitimate. We thus must consider the conditions essential to power legitimization:

> Collective approval of power legitimates that power. People who consider that the advantages they gain from a superior's exercise of power outweigh the hardships that compliance with his demands imposes on them tend to communicate to each other their [feelings of] approval of the ruler and their feelings of obligation to him.
>
> Collective disapproval of power engenders opposition. People who share the experience of being exploited by the unfair demands of those in positions of power . . . are likely to communicate their feelings of anger, frustration, and aggression to each other.[13]

Implicit in this quotation is the assumption that norms exist by which a collective judgment can be made about the fairness of the demands made. Schools, as social units reflecting the broader community, have sets of moral, cognitive, and aesthetic norms that govern the social exchanges that take place in the classrooms of any particular school. Because these norms form a critical part of the sociological context within which teachers must work to establish legitimacy, we will assume that the situation in our model is one in which there is a high degree of homogeneity about some set of values and orientations. In other words, the problems that can arise in exchange relationships due to a failure to have sent cues received because of differing value systems in operation within a classroom will not be considered in this model.

SSC and the Legitimizing Process

So far in this discussion, communication has been seen as the process whereby ideas and facts are passed from the teacher to the students. The hypothesis with which we shall be working is that there are two basic types of communication in a classroom. One is that of Subject Matter (ideas and facts), the other is Affect Communication, or the degree to which the students are aware of the teacher's personal concern for them as human beings, the degree to which the students feel that the teacher cares for them. It is hypothesized that Intuitional Role-Taking can explain the psychological process whereby a teacher is able to communicate Affect; whereas it is Inferential Role-Taking that enables a teacher to communicate ideas and facts, Subject Matter.

[13] *Ibid.*, p. 23.

The power a teacher has over his students will be collectively experienced as legitimate by his students when that teacher's *SSC* enables him to communicate some combination of Subject Matter and Affect collectively experienced as producing benefits that exceed the cost of subordination and compliance.

Implicit in Exchange Theory is the assumption that Social Man is much like his counterpart Economic Man: both are maximizers. When Social Man is in a position that gives him power, he seeks to maximize the level of legitimacy he can generate in his relationships with his followers; that is, he seeks to maximize the degree to which those who must subordinate themselves to him (comply with his demands) do so willingly. This being so, he spontaneously adjusts his leadership behavior to generate the highest level of leader-pleasing behavior in those over whom he exercises power within the constraints imposed upon him by his leadership responsibilities, the time and energy he has available to devote to a particular leadership position, and his basic abilities.

A teacher's attempt to maximize his legitimacy is critically constrained by his *SSC, ceteris paribus*. Within *ceteris paribus* is his knowledge of the subject being taught, the time and energy he can devote to teaching, and the minimum academic standards he either imposes on himself or has imposed upon him by some external agency.

Students are assumed to be such that they will produce teacher-rewarding actions in return for Subject Matter and Affect Communication. When these teacher-rewarding actions reach some critical level legitimacy results; some teachers, however, will be considered to be more legitimate in their exercise of power than are others, and, *ceteris paribus* it will be the teacher's *SSC* that determines how he can generate legitimacy.

A teacher having an *SSC* in which Intuitional Role-Taking is the dominant factor will find that he can generate Affect Communication more easily than he can Subject Matter Communication. On the other hand, a teacher having an *SSC* in which Inferential Role-Taking is the dominant factor will find that he can generate Subject Matter Communication more easily than he can Affect Communication. The amount of time and energy a teacher devotes to a class is one of the givens in the analysis. Given a teacher's *SSC*, therefore, he will find that, by devoting the determined amount of time and energy to a class, he can generate or produce, one kind of communication in larger amounts than he can another. He finds it easier to produce Affect Communication than he does Subject Matter Communication (or the other way around).

To give this notion of ease of production a more analytical base consider the following experiment: A given class of students, having homogeneity about the same values and orientations as does their teacher, is asked to score their teacher on the types of behaviors h exhibits, according to a form that has been developed for this purpose. The teacher is asked to do everything he can to communicate Subject Matter. He teaches the class for two weeks, emphasizing Subject Matter only; at the end of the period, the students score him on the behaviors he has exhibited. The collective judgment of the class is converted into an Index of Affect Communication vs. Subject Matter Communication; this is plotted on a graph in which the axes are Production of Affect Communication and Production of Subject Matter Communication. During the next two-week period, he is asked to increase his Affect Communication, while still placing emphasis on Subject Matter; he is again scored by his students and the resulting coordinate is plotted. The experiment goes on until the point is reached where the teacher is asked to communicate Affect to the exclusion of Subject Matter, insofar as this is possible. The coordinates produced through this experiment will generate what might be termed a Production Possibilities Curve for this teacher, giving all the combinations of Subject Matter and Affect Communication this teacher is capable of producing, holding time and energy constant. The Production Possibilities Curves of different teachers will differ, *ceteris paribus,* as a function of the teachers' individual *SSCs.*

The results of our hypothetical experiment are shown in Figure 14. Curve $c'c$ indicates the experimental results for a teacher having an *SSC* in which Intuitional Role-Taking dominates. For the same expenditure of time and energy, the Type C Teacher can produce a much higher level of Affect than he can Subject Matter, as these two types of communication are perceived by his students. Curve $b'b$ gives the experimental results for a teacher who spends approximately the same amount of time and energy in teaching the class as did Type C, and who has approximately the same mastery of subject as Type C, but who has an *SSC* in which Inferential Role-Taking dominates. The Type B Teacher can produce a much higher level of Subject Matter Communication than can Type C, but he is much lower in his ability to communicate Affect. Curve $a'a$ was produced experimentally by a teacher having an *SSC* that combined both Inferential and Intuitional Role-Taking. Type A cannot produce the level of Affect of a Type C, nor can he produce a level of Subject Matter of a Type B, but, as Figure 14 indicates, he can produce a number of combinations of Affect and Subject Matter Communication that are higher, in combination, than those B and C can produce.

Indifference Curve Analysis

The question now arises as to which type of *SSC,* that represented by Teacher Type A, B, or C, can produce the highest level of legitimacy and most benefit his students, where benefit is defined as aiding students

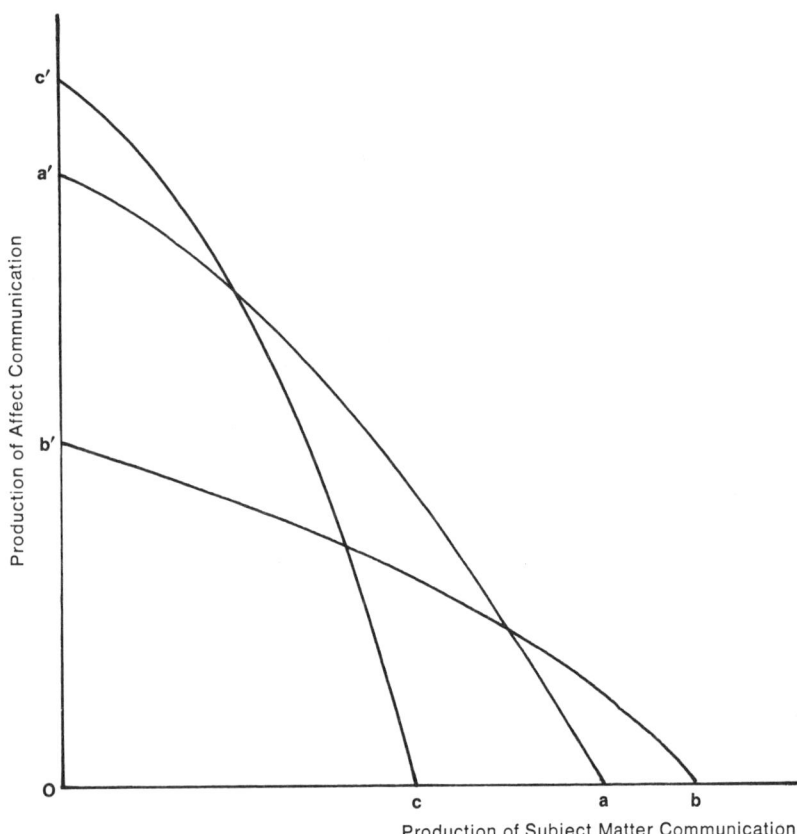

FIGURE 14. Production Possibilities Curve for Teachers of Differing SSCs

in the development of their individual potentials as well as communicating certain particular subject-related ideas and facts. At this point we are concerned with determining the level of legitimacy, and in that determination the tastes and preferences of the students must come into play.

Economists have developed a method for representing the tastes and preferences of consumers and, in a less well accepted way, of representing the tastes and preferences of a community. The technique is known as indifference curve analysis, and by using it in conjunction with the Production Possibilities Curves of Figure 14, we can determine which SSC will most likely generate the highest level of legitimacy.

An indifference curve is a graphic specification of all the combinations of two things, both of which are normally experienced as being desirable, yielding an identical level of satisfaction for the person whose tastes and preferences are being represented by the indifference curve. The slope of the indifference curve will, therefore, yield the rate at which the person in question is willing to substitute one thing for the other and still be indifferent to the substitution because the net effect of the change in combination is to leave the individual neither better nor worse off than he was before the substitution took place. To explain this idea more fully, consider the following hypothetical situation: A student is given a standardized list of teacher behaviors on which he scores his teacher. That score is converted into an index of Affect and Subject Matter Communication and is plotted, just as was done in Figure 14. That coordinate is used to divide the graph into quadrants, which have been labeled I through IV in Figure 15. Any combination of Affect and

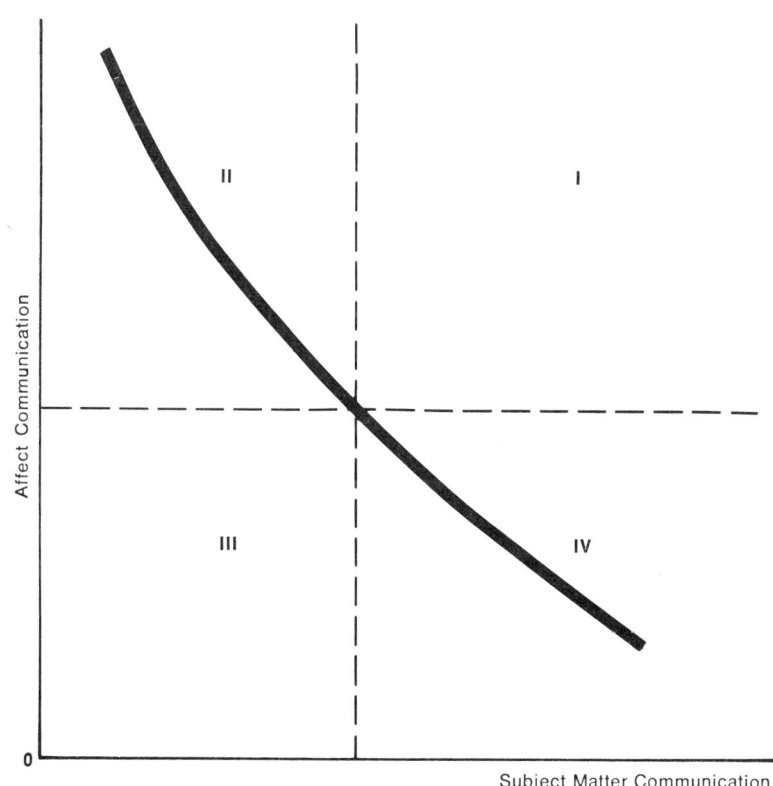

FIGURE 15. **Tastes and Preferences Shown Through Indifference Curves or Zones of Indifference**

Subject Matter Communication greater than that indicated at the origin of the quadrants will lie in Quadrant I; that is, any combination involving a higher level of both types of communication will lie within Quadrant I. It is clear that having more of both these desirable types of communication take place between the teacher and the student will be viewed by the student as an improvement in his situation. It is also evident that any movement into Quadrant III will be viewed by the student as undesirable because it involves a reduction in the level of both types of communication.

The situation in Quadrants II and IV is not so clear; in moving into either of these quadrants, the student is getting more of one type of communication and less of the other. Depending upon his individual tastes and preferences, he will feel better off than he was, worse off than he was, or indifferent, neither better nor worse off than he was at the start of the experiment.

By systematically varying the experienced combination of Affect and Subject Matter Communication, limiting the variation to points within Quadrants II and IV, it will be possible to determine his zone of indifference vis-à-vis the student's original position. Any combination lying above the zone will be one experienced by the student as an improved situation, and any combination lying below the zone will be experienced as less satisfactory than was the reference combination. By selecting reference combinations above and below the zone of indifference and by making these coordinates the origin of a new set of quadrants, indifference zones of points of equal satisfaction (but greater or less than that indicated in Figure 15) may be determined. The resulting plot of these zones of indifference, each zone of greater satisfaction than those below and to the left of it, and each containing points giving all combinations yielding a given ordinal level of satisfaction, is usually referred to as an indifference map.

Normally the indifference curves will be convex to the origin of the graph. Without becoming involved in all that is implied by convexity, the reason the curves are so shaped is that, as more of one thing is gained, the less valued is the marginal unit received relative to the value of the marginal unit of the thing traded off in moving along an indifference curve. As one moves away from the middle portion of the curve, therefore, he accumulates relatively large amounts of one thing and relatively small amounts of the other. In such circumstances, an individual will require larger and larger amounts of the abundant item to compensate for successive incremental losses of the rare item if his level of satisfaction is to be maintained. To show this kind of relationship graphically requires a convex indifference curve. The convexity property of the indifference curve is critical to the operation of the model.

A MODEL OF SPONTANEOUS MUTUAL ADJUSTMENT

Assuming that in each class a representative student can be identified, this student's indifference map illustrating his attitude toward Affect and Subject Matter Communication is determined. This map is superimposed on the Production Possibilities Curves, as shown in Figure 16. Three average or representative student's indifference curves are shown. All combinations of Affect and Subject Matter Communication identified by Curve A_1 are equally satisfactory to the representative student, and

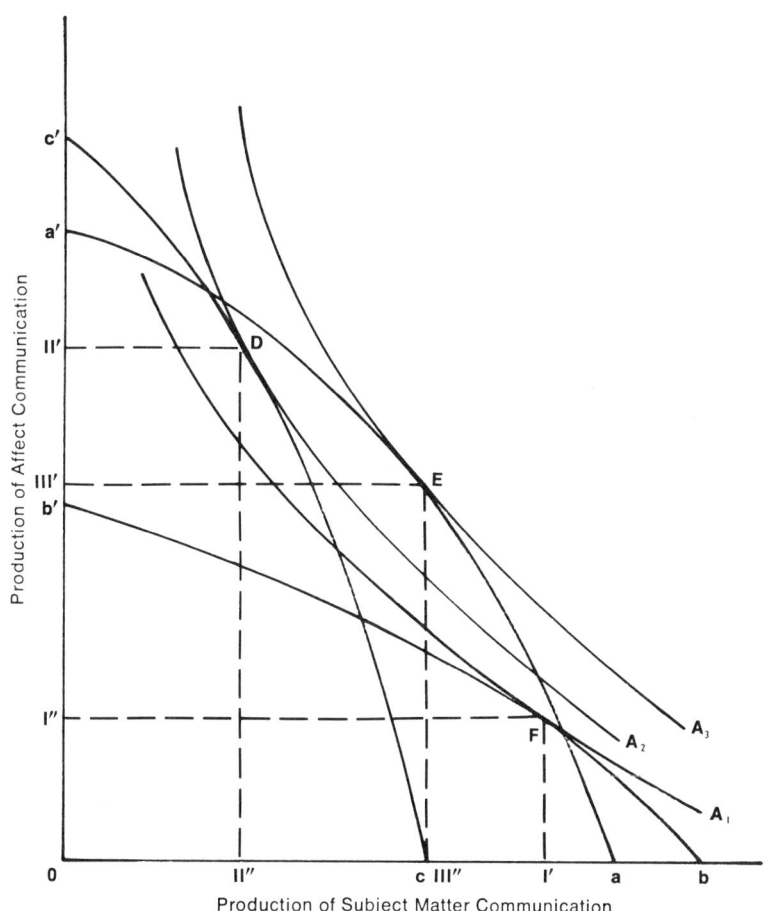

FIGURE 16. A Model of Legitimacy Determination within the Classroom Context

all are equally less satisfactory than would be any combination identified by Curve A_2. All points on A_2 are equally satisfactory, but any point on A_3 would be more satisfactory, etc.

For purposes of discussion, it is hypothesized that the A_1 level of satisfaction is not high enough to justify the sacrifices involved in enrollment in the course; a teacher who cannot generate a level of satisfaction greater than A_1 will therefore not be seen as exercising legitimate power. Teacher Type B's Production Possibilities Curve, Curve $b'b$, shows him as capable of generating any number of combinations of Affect and Subject Matter Communication, but of these it is the combination indicated by Point F that gains him the highest level of student satisfaction, and this level is not sufficiently high for him to be seen by his students as exercising legitimate power.

As Figure 16 shows, the highest level of satisfaction a teacher can generate will always come at that combination of Affect and Subject Matter Communication for which an indifference curve is tangent to the Production Possibilities Curve. As long as the Production Possibilities Curve is concave to the origin and the indifference curves are convex to the origin, a best possible point can be determined.

The best solution to the maximization problem for the Type B Teacher, Combination F, involves a combination in which Subject Matter dominates and Inferential Role-Taking is highly important. The best combination for a Type C Teacher is Combination D, a combination in which Affect dominates and Intuitional Role-Taking is critical. From this we may conclude that, given the shape of the curves, each type of teacher will do best when applying that type of role-taking characteristic of his individual *SSC*.

If the A_2 level of satisfaction is high enough to overbalance the sacrifices involved in course enrollment, Teacher Type C will be viewed as exercising legitimate power. Assuming that A_2 is sufficiently high to cause a Type C Teacher to be seen as legitimate, consider what this means in terms of the tastes and preferences of the students. In going from Combination F, an illegitimate combination, to Combination D, a legitimate combination, Subject Matter Communication has fallen from I' to II'' and Affect Communication has gone from I'' to II''. Clearly, this class has a need for, a taste for, Affect over Subject Matter. Any number of things might account for a class's needing Affect, including the age of the students (the very young need a particularistic social environment) and the home life of the students (young people coming from broken or emotionally impoverished homes seek in the school what they cannot obtain outside the school).

In Figure 16, Teacher Type A, the teacher whose *SSC* combines both types of role-taking, best meets the needs of the students as these are reflected in the indifference curve map. Combination E, involving somewhat less Subject Matter Communication than Combination F, and somewhat less Affect than Combination D, but a more balanced combination of each type of communication than either Type C or Type B can generate, meets the highest level of student approval, the A_3 level.

Social exchange involves rewards for the parties to the exchange as well as emergent properties in terms of the norms governing social intercourse that develop in the process of the exchanges between a leader and those over whom he has power. The cues sent and received in the course of social exchange between teacher and class constitute the means whereby the point of maximum satisfaction is attained, which is the point of tangency between an indifference curve and the Production Possibilities Curve. The norms that emerge as a result of this process of adjustment constitute an important educational byproduct of the adjustment process.

To explain the process of adjustment whereby a teacher comes to produce the combination of Affect and Subject Matter that maximizes student satisfaction (and thereby maximizes the teacher's legitimacy within the constraints imposed by his *SSC* and the other parametric conditions of the model), consider a situation in which the teacher is producing a non-optimal combination, such as is illustrated by Points a and c of Figure 17.

At Point a, the produced combination is relatively high on Affect and low on Subject Matter when compared to the legitimacy maximizing combination, illustrated by Point b. Students will respond to this situation by reacting in a strong positive way to any variation in the produced combination in the direction of increased Subject Matter Communication and quite weakly to any variation in the other direction. For example, any increase in applied Inferential Role-Taking, such as a more than usually elaborate set of examples in the explanation of some idea or concept, will be met with great interest and initiative on the part of the students, that is, by teacher-rewarding reactions; any display of increased Affect will be turned aside. Should the teacher be producing at Point c, the situation will be just the reverse. Any increase in produced Affect will be met with more than expected warmth, a teacher-rewarding reaction; increased Subject Matter Communication will generate apparent indifference.

Thus, through a process of spontaneous mutual adjustment, the teacher is directed along his Production Possibilities Curve toward the point of highest student satisfaction, the point of maximum legitimacy. Once the maximally satisfactory combination has been established—Point b in Figure 17—the question arises as to how this situation is signaled to the teacher. The point of maximum teacher legitimacy,

108 SOCIOECONOMIC METHODS

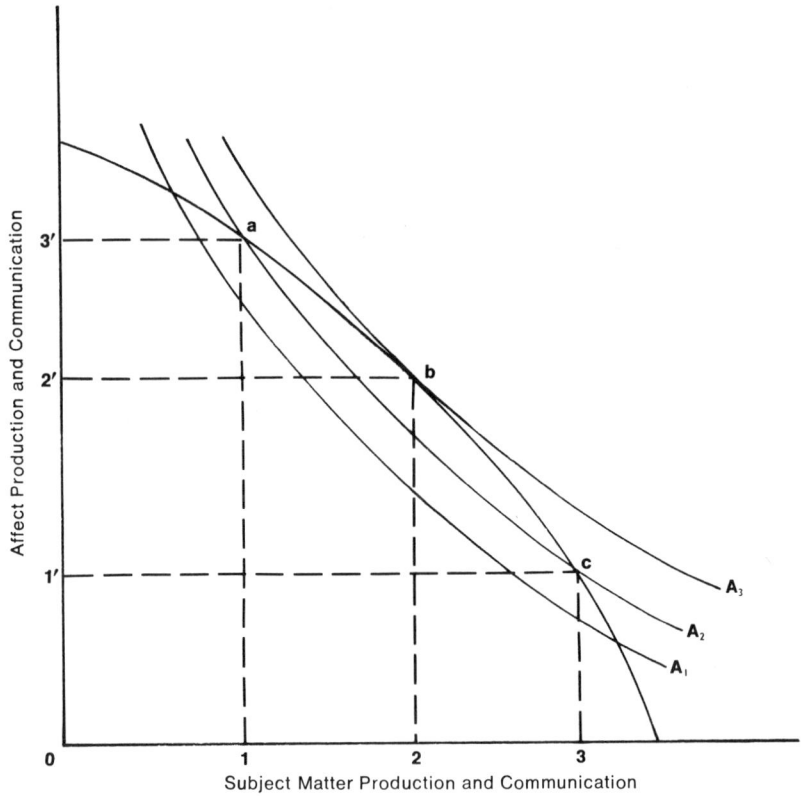

FIGURE 17. The Process of Spontaneous Mutual Adjustment

which in some cases may be a level of satisfaction inadequate to legitimate the teacher's power, is indicated by the absence of any differential response on the part of students to any change in the produced combination.

Legitimacy Maximization and the Dilemma of Leadership

There are certain conditions under which a teacher will *not* seek to maximize his legitimacy. We now direct our analysis of spontaneous mutual adjustment to the consideration of one such condition. Legitimacy maximization is constrained not only by the interaction of the tastes and preferences of the students with the Production Possibilities Curve of the teacher, but also by the Subject Matter standards the teacher sets for himself in recognition of the long-run interests of his students, or are set by some external agent. When the standard is set by the teacher's own sense of responsibility to his students, the teacher is faced with what Blau refers to as the dilemma of leadership:

> . . . preoccupation with the approval of followers [students] interferes with a leader's [teacher's] ability to command their respect and compliance by making the greatest contribution to their welfare he can, because concern with being liked prevents him from basing his decisions consistently on criteria of effectiveness alone. Such preoccupation, in other words, induces a leader [teacher] sometimes to refrain from making what is the best decision in his judgment for fear of antagonizing subordinates.[14]

EMERGENT PROPERTIES OF EXCHANGE RELATIONSHIPS UNDER LEGITIMATE AND ILLEGITIMATE POWER CONDITIONS

Inasmuch as resolution of the dilemma of leadership depends upon a social psychological process whereby students are influenced to change their tastes and preferences, their attitudes regarding their need for Subject Matter Communication, some discussion of the relevant research in social psychology is called for.

Allen E. Bergin attempts to demonstrate "that the conditions of persuasive communication known to produce attitude changes regarding issues external to one's self are applicable to self-relevant attitudes . . . ."[15] The variables in Bergin's experiment were the degree of dissonance of the communication and the credibility of the communicator. In his summary of results, Bergin states:

> This experiment tested the effect of persuasive communications upon S's [Subjects'] conceptions of their masculinity-femininity. Communications were varied in terms of discrepancy and communicator credibility [where discrepancy refers to the difference between the Subject's present attitude and the attitude the communicator wishes the Subject to accept concerning an aspect of the self], and hypotheses about attitude change were formulated in terms of Festinger's dissonance theory. S's changed their self-ratings as a consequence of the . . . communications in conformity with the hypotheses. Amount of change increased as a

---
[14] *Ibid.*, p. 203.
[15] Allen E. Bergin, "The Effect of Dissonant Persuasive Communications upon Changes in a Self-Referring Attitude," *Journal of Personality, 30* (September 1962), p. 423.

monotonic function of discrepancy under high-credibility conditions in contrast to little or no change under low-credibility conditions.[16]

The self-conception Bergin selected for modification is one that it may be supposed would be highly resistant to change, perhaps more so than an individual's attitude toward his need for ideas and facts (his need for Subject Matter Communication). Converting Bergin's terms into those that have been used here, a teacher viewed by the class as exercising legitimate power is a high-credibility communicator, whereas a teacher viewed as illegitimate would be treated by the students as a low-credibility communicator.

Bergin's results are shown in Figure 18, where Mean Attitude Change is plotted as a function of the two control variables. In the high-credibility mode, Mean Change increases as a function of increasing discrepancy; in the low-credibility mode, it decreases as a function of increasing discrepancy.

Figure 19 illustrates a situation in which a teacher determines that it is in the students' best interest that he produce a combination of Affect and Subject Matter different from one that would maximize his legitimacy. The maximum legitimacy point, T^1, is the point of tangency between the indifference curve, curve A^1, representing the students' attitude on their Affective versus Subject Matter needs, and the teacher's Production Possibilities Curve. The combination the teacher produces is indicated by Point T^2, which has coordinates A^*S^*. The teacher sacrifices some legitimacy in producing the T^2 combination, but not so much that he is in any danger of losing his legitimacy.

The impact of the teacher's producing combination T^2 instead of T^1 is to signal to the students a discrepancy between their attitudes and his about the level of Subject Matter Communication that best fits their needs. The teacher must deny the cues they send regarding their Affective needs and persist in the determined level of Subject Matter Communication, Level S^*, even though he earns little or no reward for movements in the direction of increased Subject Matter Communication. Because of the teacher's legitimacy, the students will receive his dissonant message as a call for attitudinal change—change in the direction of an increased sense of personal need for Subject Matter and a reduced need for Affect Communication. According to the research findings, students can be expected to adjust to the discrepancy by altering their attitudes in the direction indicated by the high-credibility communicator, the legitimate teacher. This change in attitudes, which is supposed to take place over the course of the year, is indicated graphically by Indifference

[16] *Ibid.*, p. 437.

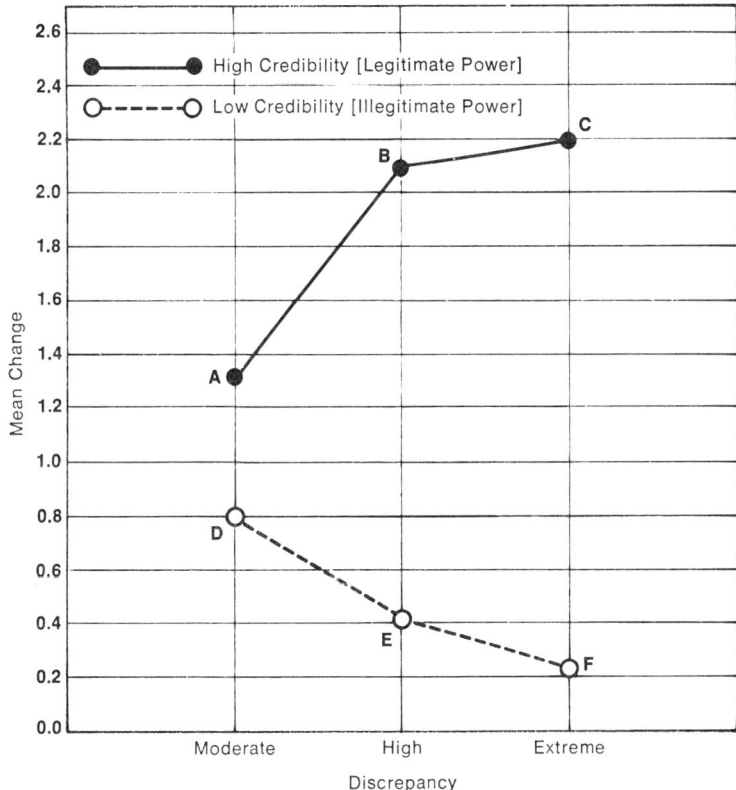

FIGURE 18. Mean Change in Self-Attitudes as a Function of Communicator Credibility and Communication Discrepancy (adapted from Bergin)

Curve A^1, which becomes steeper and shifts toward the origin. The new indifference curve is labeled Curve A^2; it represents the same, or approximately the same, level of satisfaction as that represented by Curve A^1. In other words, Curve A^1 becomes Curve A^2 because of induced attitudinal change.

The only possible way of resolving the dilemma of leadership is to induce attitudinal change on the part of the followers. The teacher in our model, who is a Type A Teacher, one using both Inferential and Intuitional Role-Taking modes, has successfully resolved the dilemma and has resolved it in a way consistent with his educational task. The teacher will be rewarded for his persistance by an increasing sense of

112   SOCIOECONOMIC METHODS

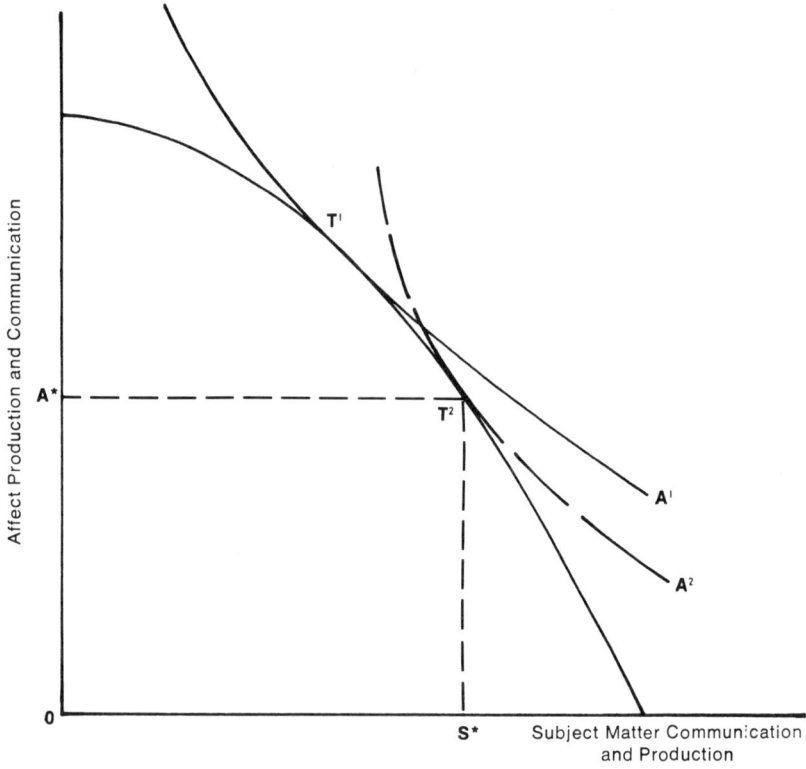

FIGURE 19. Attitude Change under Legitimate Leadership

his own legitimacy as a teacher as attitudes shift over the course of the year.

What can be said about teachers of Type C, the Intuitional Role-Taking teacher, and Type B, the Inferential Role-Taking teacher? Because these two types are most likely to operate at low levels of legitimacy, they are unlikely to be capable of resolving the dilemma of leadership. Because they have low credibility, they will be unable to induce attitudinal shifts within their students. Furthermore, because their legitimacy is low to begin with, they often will feel that they cannot afford further reductions in legitimacy by producing any combination of Affect and Subject Matter Communication other than one that maximizes their legitimacy. This situation may be particularly damaging to the long-run interests of students enrolled in a class led by a Type C Teacher, because he must maximize legitimacy by producing very high levels of Affect Communication. The long-run effects of the Type B

Teacher, on the other hand, may be expected to be less injurious due to his maximizing legitimacy (or minimizing illegitimacy) at high levels of Subject Matter Communication, as indicated in Figure 16, a determination that rests on considerations dealing with the level of education—primary, secondary, or tertiary—involved.

Because of their *SSC*s, teachers develop images or personality types as, in part, an emergent property of their ability to resolve the dilemma of leadership. In other words, teachers attempt to reflect to their students a personality type or image in keeping with the situation their *SSC* creates within the classroom; thus the impression students may have of a teacher and the impression others have of the individual in his non-teaching statuses can differ widely.

In Figure 20, we show a four-fold diagram in which teaching per-

	High Academic Demands	Low Academic Demands
High Need for Student Approval	*Genuine Educator* SSC characterized by a combined use of both intuitional and inferential role-taking Social and Spatial Knowledge Type *A*	*Good Guy* SSC characterized by a dependence upon intuitional role-taking Social Knowledge *Gemeinschaft* Type *C*
Low Need for Student Approval	*Task Master* SSC characterized by a dependence upon inferential role-taking Spatial Knowledge *Gesellschaft* Type *B*	*Unpredictable* SSC characterized by an inability to practice role-taking; thus, he cannot establish a social exchange with his students

FIGURE 20. Personality Type as a Function of *SSC*

sonalities are associated with different types of *SSC*. Just as there were two basic types of communication hypothesized to go on within a classroom, there are two basic personality components in a teaching personality, one matched with each type of communication.

A teacher having an *SSC* in which Inferential Role-Taking dominates can be expected to project to his students a personality in keeping with the high academic demands he must make to maximize his legitimacy (or minimize his illegitimacy). In addition, such a teacher, because he is incapable of producing Affect, will reflect a personality attitude consistent with a low need for student approval. This teacher is *B* Type; he will be most effective as an educator when placed with students having very high Subject Matter needs. We call this type The Task Master.

A teacher having an *SSC* in which Intuitional Role-Taking dominates can be expected to show a personality to his students in which he combines low academic demands with a high need for student approval. This teacher will be effective with students having unusually high Affective needs. He is the Type *C* Teacher and is known to students as a Good Guy.

There is one type of teacher that does not fit into our analysis because this teacher really does not enter into an ongoing social exchange with his students. He is something like the kindergarten teacher cited earlier in this chapter. This teacher often will project an image to his students that combines low academic demands with low need for student approval. Students may characterize such a teacher as Unpredictable.

The last of the four types is Type *A,* the teacher who combines both Inferential and Intuitional Role-Taking modes. His teaching personality will communicate to his students his high academic demands and his high need for student approval. He will be thought of as a Genuine Educator. A quotation from the 1957 postscript to Buber's *I and Thou* not only illustrates how a Genuine Educator makes use of both Inferential and Intuitional Role-Taking modes, but it also supports, from a philosophical prospective, the point we have made about the ability of the Genuine Educator to induce a shift in self-attitudes within his students:

> In order to help the realization of the best potentialities in the pupil's life, the teacher must really mean *him* as the definite person he is in his potentiality and his actuality; more precisely, he must not know him as a mere sum of qualities, strivings and inhibitions [that is, he must not know him only through Inferential Role-Taking], he must be aware of him as a whole being and affirm him in this wholeness. But he can only do this if he meets him

again and again as his partner in a bipolar situation. And in order that his effect upon him may be a unified and significant one he must also live this situation, again and again, in all its moments not merely from his own end but also from that of his partner; he must practice the kind of realization which I call inclusion (*Umfassung*) [that is, he must practice Intuitional Role-Taking].[17]

In the light of our discussion and of Buber's statement, consider Piaget's meaning in the following:

> It is idle, again, to try and transform the child's mind from the outside, when his own taste for active research and his desire for cooperation suffice to ensure a normal intellectual development. The adult must therefore be a collaborator and not a master, from this double point of view, moral and rational.[18]

The moral component Piaget calls for requires Affect Communication, which requires Intuitional Role-Taking, whereas the rational component requires Inferential Role-Taking. When the two are practiced together, the result is genuine education from both Buber's and Piaget's points of view.

IMPLICATIONS OF THE MODEL FOR CLASS SIZE

One of the most vexing questions in the whole of pedagogy is that of the ideal or optimal class size. To the degree that social exchange is difficult to establish in a large lecture-type setting, our analysis would indicate that little genuine education is likely to take place under such conditions; that is, little induced change in self-attitudes will likely be accomplished. Some teachers, however, do appear to have an *SSC* that combines both Role-Taking modes with an unusual ability to project Affect to large numbers of students, regardless of distance from the teacher. On the basis of limited personal experience with such teachers, the success of the projection appears to be a function of the degree of value homogeneity between teacher and class as well as the degree to which the teacher's need for student approval leads him to make himself available outside class. There is a large amount of published research

---

[17] Martin Buber, *I and Thou* (New York: Scribner, 1957), quoted in Stark, "*Gemeinschaft*," p. 200.
[18] Jean Piaget, "Social Factors in Moral Development," from *The Moral Judgment of the Child* (London: Routledge & Kegan Paul Ltd., 1932), reprinted in H. Proshansky and B. Seidenberg, eds., *Basic Studies in Social Psychology* (New York: Holt, Rinehart and Winston, 1965), p. 281.

that could be brought to bear on this question within the context of the model presented in this chapter; that task will not be undertaken here, however.

METHODOLOGICAL CONSIDERATIONS

The method used in structuring the logic of this analysis appears to differ greatly from that utilized in all previous models. In the case of this model, appearances do not deceive; the method does represent a change from that previously applied. The use of economic constructs, such as indifference and production possibility curves, has enabled us to make an integrated use of theoretical structures from sociology and social psychology, but the integrating technique, like a catalyst, only facilitated the interaction of the two, while itself remaining unchanged.

Generally speaking, most previous efforts to explore the subject matters of other disciplines utilizing techniques drawn from economics have been of a catalytic nature when well done and, when not well done, have been no more than translations from one discipline's terminology into another's. In our view, for the operation to be legitimate, the product of the combination must be something more than could be accomplished by any discipline alone. Having suggested a criterion, the reader may judge the legitimacy of the method applied, a method that only approximates a socioeconomic analysis of classroom communication.

POSTSCRIPT

A point that has been stressed throughout this book is that the socioeconomic method is in no way tied to the application that has been made of it in this work; that is, although it was determined to draw the applications from education, the method is in no way limited to the analysis of problems that arise in the education problem setting. The value of the method is in the way in which it aids model construction across a broad range of social science disciplines, a value that derives from the way in which the methods of economics have been generalized to serve the needs of the other social sciences. What has been done goes beyond generalization toward integration, however, and it is, perhaps, this matter of integration that is at once both the strength and the weakness of the kind of work that has been done here.

SOME POSSIBLE PROBLEMS

During the academic year 1954-55, Kenneth E. Boulding completed the manuscript of a book he was to title *The Image: Knowledge in Life and*

Society. In this book, Boulding set forward an interesting notion: Men behave in accord with the image they have of existential reality. Messages received from those holding other images are, generally, not capable of reception and, not being received (understood) will not, therefore, influence or alter their existential reality. Image fusion or transformation does go on, however, mainly because it is so very difficult to maintain barriers between one subculture (and its private "image"), one subuniverse of discourse, and the rest of the world's subcultures. To extend this thought, Boulding notes that:

> Once, however, the barriers which divide subcultures are broken, messages are received from other subcultures which are inconsistent with the images held in one. The reaction to this situation is either rapid re-establishment of the barriers between the subcultures or it is a rapid change in the images of all of them. The extraordinary rapidity with which images have changed in the last two hundred years is perhaps mainly a result of increased communication among previously isolated subcultures. It is easy to overestimate, however, the extent of this breakdown of isolation. As we have seen, in the intellectual subculture, isolation actually seems to be increasing because of the development of specialization and the compartmentalization of language.[1]

Insofar as the socioeconomic method is successful, it must result in increased communication between the social science disciplines. And, if it is successful, it will be because it brings about a fusion of images, resulting in a modified or new image. The problem that then arises is one to which Boulding alerts us: will the new image be received? That is, is there a place for the products of interdisciplinary social theory, the sort of theory our method is intended to generate? Many ventures in multidisciplinary and interdisciplinary work have had small impact on the course of social research because they could not overcome the reception problem. Boulding's book is, itself, but one example. Others might include Polanyi's work in economic anthropology, particularly his *Great Transformation;* Dahl and Lindblom's *Politics, Economics and Welfare;* and Parsons' attempts to fuse economics and sociology. The "communication problem," as this writer has come to think of it, has been very much in mind as the writing here developed.

In selecting the material to be used in this study, some care was taken to draw from all the social sciences, with at least one chapter depending

---

[1] Kenneth E. Boulding, *The Image: Knowledge in Life and Society* (Ann Arbor: The University of Michigan Press, 1961), p. 146.

heavily upon constructs drawn from economics, Chapter VII, "A Socioeconomic Model of Classroom Communication"; one chapter built from the concerns of political science, Chapter III, "Literacy in a Model of Low-Level Equilibrium"; one chapter devoted to the construction of a socioeconomic model out of constructs drawn from social psychology, Chapter VI, "A Model of Organizational Development Applied to a School"; one chapter building from psychological constructs, Chapter IV, "A Socioeconomic Model of the Determinants of the Conceptual Level of the Curriculum"; and, of course, almost all chapters drew extensively from formal sociology. Although each discipline represents a distinct subuniverse of discourse, it was part of the design of the work that each should be made to appear as a portion of one universe, one image; for in truth they are: Each discipline posits functional relationships, each posits complex chains of causality, and, thus, each is capable of producing geometric constructions that look like the constructions produced by the others. Equilibrium is a perfectly general concept, equally useful in theory generation to all, as are the notions of required system states and actual system states; the path followed from an actual to a required state; system stability; non-equilibrium process systems; objective function specification; and the model-based strategy of the normatively inclined investigator, to name but a few of the components encompassed by the socioeconomic method.

CONCLUSIONS

In the preceding section of this Postscript, we raised a question that was only indirectly answered: Is there a place for interdisciplinary social theory? Our answer (and this book may be seen as a statement of this answer) is that there is small likelihood that interdisciplinary work in the social sciences will find a place in social research before there is a more general acceptance of some means whereby the results of work in each discipline can be presented in a format that is more nearly universal. Because it is a method adequate to the range of demands made by the various disciplines, socioeconomic model construction may prove to be a building block in the direction of improved inter-disciplinary communication.

INDEX OF NAMES

Ackley, Gardner, 6
Adelman, Irma, 33
Anderson, C. A., 18
Bandura, Albert, 91
Bergin, Allen E., 109, 110
Blau, Peter M., 90, 96, 97, 109
Blaug, Mark, 20
Bos, Hendricks C., 6n, 10, 13
Boulding, Kenneth, 117, 118
Buber, Martin, 114, 115
Cohen, A., 87
Coleman, James S., 18, 95
Cooley, Charles Horton, 64, 96
Cressler, D. L., 91
Dahl, Robert, 118
Denison, Edward, 18
Durkheim, Emile, 60
Fairweather, G. W., 90, 91
Festinger, L., 109
Floud, Jean, 18
Foster, P. J., 20
Gouldner, Alvin, 17, 20
Hagen, Everett E., 31
Halsey, A. H., 18
Harbison, Frederick, 19, 33

Harris, Seymour E., 24n
Harvey, O. J., 50
Homans, George C., 96
Hornstein, Harvey, 82
Hunt, D. E., 50
Jencks, Christopher, 61
Kahn, R. L., 83, 86
Kelley, Harold H., 96
Keynes, John M., 35
Ladinsky, Jack, 48
Lawrence, Paul R., 82
Lehman, Stanley, 86
Leibenstein, Harvey, 35
Lerner, Daniel, 18, 32, 33, 34, 36, 38
Lindblom, Charles, 118
Lorsch, Jay W., 82
Machlup, Fritz, 22, 28, 29, 30, 57
Malinowski, Bronislaw, 32
Mansfield, Edwin, 22
Maynard, H., 91
McClelland, David, 32
Merton, Robert K., 25
Morris, Cynthia Taft, 33
Myers, Charles A., 19, 33
Parsons, Talcott, 7, 22, 26, 58, 95, 118

INDEX OF NAMES

Pervin, Lawrence A., 60
Piaget, Jean, 115
Polanyi, Karl, 118
Quinn, R. P., 83, 86
Riesman, David, 61
Rist, Ray C., 97
Rogoff, Natalie, 95
Rostow, W. W., 32, 33
Sanders, D. H., 91
Schroder, Harold M., 50
Schumpeter, Joseph, 3n
Shimkunas, A. M., 88
Smelser, Neil J., 58

Smith, Adam, 10
Snoek, J. D., 83, 86
Stark, Stanley, 96n
Stern, George C., 49
Stigler, George J., 28, 29
Stotland, E., 87
Thibaut, John W., 96
Tinbergen, Jan, 6, 10, 13
Toennies, Ferdinand, 96
Tuckman, Bruce W., 60
Tullock, Gordon, 57, 58
Wirth, Louis, 7
Wolfe, D. M., 83, 86, 87, 95

INDEX OF SUBJECTS

Admissions
  selectivity of, 61, 68ff., 76
Anxiety, 86ff., 92
Attitude Change, 86, 110ff.

Change, 20ff., 85
  Social, 22ff.
  Technological, 22ff.
  Urban, 85
  Model-Guided Strategy of, 20
Change Agent, 82ff., 88, 92ff.
Classroom, 95
  size of class, 115ff.
Cognitive Style, 50
Cognitive Structuring, 50, 86
  definition of, 86-87
  need-for-cognition, 86
Collaborative Behavior, 83ff., 87
Communication, 25, 33, 50, 74, 78, 95
  conceptual level of, 50
  sociological style of, 95ff.
  affect communication, 99ff.
  subject matter communication, 99ff.
  sociology of, 95
Community, 66, 73, 76

Comparative Method, 32-33
Compression
  poetic, 51
  resistance to, 51
Creative Process, 64n
Crisis Situation, 86, 92
Critical Minimum Effort Thesis, 35
Curriculum, 18, 24ff., 30ff., 46
  conceptual level of, 50ff., 59, 75
  in *The Republic*, 13

Development, 19, 32

Education
  in *The Republic*, 5, 6-7, 13
Emergent Properties, 31, 39, 88, 90, 95, 107, 113
Enrollment, 74, 76
Equilibrium, 21-22, 27ff., 55, 64, 71, 92ff., 119

Faculty, 61ff., 65ff.
Functional Prerequisites, 21, 26, 95

General Studies, 24, 26

INDEX OF SUBJECTS

Geographic Mobility, 48
Gross National Product, 77

Harmony, 53, 59
   maximization of, 60ff., 64, 78
Hierarchy
   administrative, 57
   centralized control of, 65
   of objectives, 56
   structure of, 89
   top administration, 68, 70

Institution of Higher Education, 55ff., 58, 92
Indifference Curve, 101ff.
Instability, 4
Interdisciplinary Social Science, 118ff.

Kindergarten, 97
Knowledge, 59, 61, 91

Leadership, 87ff., 100
   dilemma of, 108ff.
   legitimation of, 91
Learning, 51ff., 59

Message Comprehension, 85ff., 87
Microsocietal Analysis, 45ff., 53, 57, 66, 92
Model, 28ff., 33, 35, 46
   definitions of, 3, 6
   dynamics of, 29
   kinds of, 4, 19, 35, 40
Money, 4, 12

Norms, 22, 86, 89, 99, 107

Objective Function
   definition of, 53, 54ff., 56ff.
Ockham's Razor, 38
Organization Development
   definition of, 81ff.
Organization Theory, 46, 57

Parameters, 8, 21, 28-29, 37-38, 55, 56, 69-70, 76, 82, 92, 107
Path Analysis, 63ff., 67
Pattern Maintenance, 58-59, 62ff.
Personality Types, 113
   genuine educator, 114
   good guy, 114
   task master, 114
   unpredictable, 114
Plato, 18, 21-22, 27, 31
Population, 7, 8, 10-11, 34, 38
   college age, 74

Power
   social exchange, 98ff.
   legitimate, 98ff.
Prestige, 27, 56, 59
   definition of, 58
   maximization of, 61, 66ff., 78
Production Possibilities Curve, 102ff.
Production Function
   definition of, 59
   in higher education, 59, 73
Profit, 29, 55
Psychic Mobility, 33-34
Public Goods, 4, 7, 12, 34
Planners, 20

Research, 70, 85
Role
   role sending, 85
   role ambiguity, 83ff., 86
   role taking, 96, 99
      inferential mode of, 96
      intuitional mode of, 96

Selectivity, 48ff.
Self-esteem, 83
Shah of Iran, 38
Social Change, 20, 22, 25, 31
Social Exchange, 89, 95ff., 107
   definition of, 90
   theory of, 100
Social Psychology, 82-83, 109
Socialization, 36, 39, 59, 61
Socioeconomic Analysis, 16-17, 21, 45, 57, 71, 117
Solidarity
   mechanical, 60, 61, 65
   organic, 60, 61
Specialization, 4, 8, 22, 24, 30
Spontaneous Mutual Adjustment, 55, 105ff.
Sputnik Episode, 74
Stability
   of equilibrium, 13, 40-41
   of home and community, 53
   in *The Republic*, 4-5
Statistical Verification
   of a model, 63ff., 71
Status, 22, 49
Status Set, 25
Structural-Functional Analysis, 7n

Teacher, 90, 96
   certification requirements of, 49
   demand for, 46
   quality of, 48ff., 49n
   mobility of, 48

INDEX OF SUBJECTS

Teacher—Contd
  salaries of, 46, 48
  supply of, 46
Teacher Corps, 38
Tenure, 70
Third World Nations, 32
Token Economy, 90

Unanticipated Consequences, 22
University, 27ff., 46, 56, 59, 67, 75
Utility, 54-55

Urbanization, 8, 12, 33ff.
  definition of, 7

Valid Information, 92
Values, 58, 60
Value Homogeneity, 60, 67-68, 70, 99
Vietnam War, 74

Welfare Maximization, 55, 77ff.
World Bank, 37